The Making of Bill Knapp

Also by William B. Friedricks

Henry E. Huntington and the Creation of Southern California

Covering Iowa: The History of the Des Moines Register and Tribune Company, 1849-1985

In for the Long Haul: The Life of John Ruan

Investing in Iowa: The Life and Times of F.M. Hubbell

The Real Deal: The Life of Bill Knapp

Constructing a Legacy: The Weitz Company and the Family Who Built It

A Great State Fair: The Blue Ribbon Foundation and the Revival of the Iowa State Fair

Unstoppable: The Nine Lives of Roxanne Barton Conlin

The Making of Bill Knapp

William B. Friedricks

bpc

The Making of Bill Knapp is published by Business Publications Corporation Inc., an Iowa corporation.

Copyright © 2021 by William B. Friedricks.

Reproduction or other use, in whole or in part, of the contents without permission of the publisher is strictly prohibited.

ISBN-13: 978-1-950790-06-7
Library of Congress Control Number: 2021901043
Business Publications Corporation Inc., Des Moines, IA

Cover photo courtesy of John Holtorf.

Business Publications Corporation Inc.
The Depot at Fourth
100 4th Street
Des Moines, Iowa 50309
(515) 288-3336

In memory of my dad, Burt Friedricks

CONTENTS

Preface **ix**
Acknowledgments **xiii**
Introduction **3**

Part 1. Bill Knapp's Top 10 Business Tenets

1. "Do What You Like, and It Will Never Be Work" **12**
2. "You Can't Do It All by Yourself" **16**
3. "Build Relationships and Keep in Touch" **19**
4. "Buy and Hold Land" **22**
5. "Don't Dwell on the Past; If You Do, You Lose Focus on the Present" **27**
6. "Close Deals Quickly, and Aim for a Win-Win" **30**
7. "Don't Hold Grudges" **33**
8. "Real Estate Is Risky: Do What You Can to Decrease Risks" **37**
9. "Be Prepared for Bad Times" **39**
10. "Court the Media" **41**

Part 2. Where Credit Is Due

11. Irene Knapp **46**
12. Kenny Grandquist **51**

13. Paul Knapp **56**
14. John R. Grubb **60**
15. Hy-Vee Food Stores **64**
16. Bill Wimer and Connie Wimer **68**
17. Jack Wahlig **72**
18. Harold Hughes **75**
19. John Ruan **80**
20. Guido Fenu **85**
21. Ed Campbell and Bonnie Campbell **89**
22. Dwayne McAninch **94**
23. David Kruidenier **99**
24. Roger Brooks **104**
25. Mike Knapp **109**
26. Bill Knapp II and Gerry Neugent **112**
27. Jim Cownie **117**
28. Ginny Haviland and Roger Knapp **122**
29. Greg Abel **128**
30. Susan Knapp **133**

A Note on Sources **139**
Notes **141**
Index **161**

PREFACE

In 2019, as they had done for twenty-six years, Bill and Susan Knapp hosted their annual holiday party on the first Friday of December at their sprawling ranch home. As always, the event's invitation list read like a who's who of greater Des Moines, and as usual, it was a lavish affair with fine food and drink, sumptuous desserts, and live music wafting through the air. Both Bill and Susan were terrific hosts, but as Bill made clear, "the party is and has been Susan's doing all along."[1]

That get-together, however, was different from their previous Christmas galas. It was the last one. "We've had a good run," Susan told me, "but it's time to call it quits."[2] Bill had turned ninety-three that past July, and hosting the large event was losing its allure. For many years this party, as well as all the other social functions he attended, had been opportunities to do business. Bill had liked nothing better than nailing down deals with friends or colleagues at such gatherings. But the aging business titan was slowing down, and now Bill often spent his time at these occasions reminiscing about past deals with old friends.

He certainly had a full life and career to review. After initially struggling to find his calling, he stumbled into the real estate business, which proved to be highly fertile ground. Here his penchant for constant activity was rewarded. As if playing a real-life Monopoly game, Bill was consumed by moving from project to project and wheeling and dealing. Whether buying and selling properties, developing land, or building homes, apartments, hotels, and commercial structures, he was a man on the move. More and more success led him to think about giving back, and again as if playing Monopoly, he became interested in the community chest, giving away millions to local and statewide nonprofits. "I loved the action," he observed. "The money was good, too, but it was closing the deal that motivated me. And I had no interest in resting on my laurels. I had to keep moving."[3]

Although most people start to look back and reflect on their lives as they age, this was new for Bill. He often used to rib me about my focus on the past. "You live back there," he would jest. "But you're a historian and that's good for what you do. I, however, don't dwell there. I stay in the present and keep an eye to the future." This lighthearted comment was revelatory, and for decades Bill had done exactly that. He was as good as anyone at staying in the moment and concentrating on a particular transaction. But at the same time, he also had an uncanny ability to peer into the future, frequently envisioning the impact of a deal for years to come. Yet when the deal was done, Bill filed it away, almost as if it had not happened, and was off to the next project. This ability helped make him one of the premier land developers and wealthiest business figures in the city.[4]

Bill still likes the action, still looks at properties, and still makes occasional purchases, but cutting deals is no longer a major part of his life. He continues to make significant charitable donations and remains interested in both local and national Democratic politics, but more of his time is spent looking back and assessing his life, and he is perfectly content. "If I felt any better, I'd be jealous of myself," he recently joked.[5]

This book grew out of Bill's newfound interest in reflection. In early summer of 2018, he and I were catching up over lunch at Nick's Bar and Grill in Clive, then his favorite place for a midday meal. We had been friends since 2010, when I began researching and writing his biography, *The Real Deal: The Life of Bill Knapp*, which came out in 2013. Our conversations ranged widely, but several times Bill referred to business lessons he had learned over his career. As we continued talking over lunch, Bill mentioned more principles that had led to his success.[6]

Our discussion stuck in my mind, and a couple of weeks later I scheduled another meeting with Bill. He picked up where he had left off, talking about important ideas he had come across over the years. "When I started out, I knew I was green," he later recalled, "and I was eager to learn anything I could to sell homes, purchase properties, and do deals. I kept my eyes and ears open because I thought I could learn something from just about anyone. I still believe that."[7]

This time, I scribbled down notes as Bill talked. I had heard all these thoughts years earlier when I was interviewing Bill for the biography, and I knew how important they had been in shaping the way he had operated. But now they appeared as a list of lessons, and I began to see them in a new light.

Bill and I talked a few more times that summer and fall, but he had shifted gears, emphasizing that no matter how many business lessons he had mastered, he had not made it on his own. He clearly understood that many good friends, partners, colleagues, and employees had helped him build his lucrative career. There was, however, a smaller group of people who had been essential to his success. "A lot of people have been part of it, and I always try to give those who helped me get where I am the credit they deserve." I stopped Bill right there. "Hold that thought," I said. "I think I have an idea."[8]

"What if I put together a slim volume sharing the business lessons you learned through experience and then added essays about the key people who were vital to your success?" Bill smiled. "That," he said, "would be a damn good thing."[9]

Thus, this book. Over the next year and a half, I talked frequently with Bill, nephew Bill Knapp II, and Gerry Neugent, who have worked closely with him since the 1970s and know his career better than anyone. I also interviewed others, reread my notes from my earlier work on Bill's biography, did additional research, and reviewed numerous issues of the *Des Moines Register* and *Des Moines Tribune*.

Bill and I boiled down fourteen or fifteen of his business principles to a core ten, and then we moved on to people who had been particularly significant to his career. Some were obvious, some not, but by the end of our discussions we agreed that the twenty-three people and one company included here stood out as key to his success.

Bill Knapp remains an iconic figure in Iowa's business and philanthropic communities. Clearly, his entrepreneurial drive, hard work, determination, and knack for the deal propelled him forward in the world of real estate. Equally as important, his interest in and willingness to adopt new ideas and strategies led him to piece together a number of noteworthy business tenets that guided him throughout his career. Maybe the most important of these lessons taught him that he could not succeed alone, and Bill therefore tirelessly networked, seeking out others who could help him attain his vision or who offered new opportunities.

Bill's legacy looms large over central Iowa. Whether through the real estate powerhouse of Iowa Realty, the many commercial and residential subdivisions he developed, his successful efforts to revitalize Des Moines's downtown and the Drake neighborhood, or his generous donations to many area nonprofits—several of which have named buildings in his honor—Bill has made an indelible impact on the region. He has made greater Des Moines a better place to live and work, and while he has amassed a fortune over his career, he has lived up to his adage: "You have to do good by doing good."[10]

ACKNOWLEDGMENTS

This project grew out of conversations Bill Knapp and I had over the past couple of years. Thank you, Bill, for inspiring this book and giving me the opportunity to write it.

Throughout this project, I benefited from the generosity and support of many people. Bill Knapp II and Gerry Neugent provided insight and perspective and fleshed out details. Carly Fisher put me in touch with key individuals and tracked down photographs. Susan Knapp and Ginny and Mark Haviland helped in a variety of ways. Special thanks to all of you. I could not have done this book without your assistance.

At Simpson College, Daryl Sasser, Linda Sinclair, and my undergraduate assistant, Kenzie Jeter, provided extra help with the Iowa History Center so I could focus on this book.

I had another great experience working with Business Publications Corporation. Emily Schultz capably oversaw the project from start to finish, and I again had the pleasure of working with editor Holly Carver; all writers should be so lucky.

I also had the advantage of having Jackie Crawford in my corner. As always, she read several versions of the manuscript and made each one better. Thank you, Jackie, for your careful reading, enthusiastic support, love, and understanding.

Finally, I want to dedicate this book to the memory of my father, Burt Friedricks, who unexpectedly passed away in November 2019. He had heard a lot about Bill Knapp over the years and always wanted to meet him. Sadly, he never got the chance.

The Making of Bill Knapp

INTRODUCTION

For nearly seventy years, Bill Knapp has been making things happen in greater Des Moines, shaping and reshaping the landscape by founding Iowa Realty and selling homes, buying and selling properties, developing residential subdivisions and commercial parks, and leading the effort to revitalize the city's downtown. Success in the real estate business has made him wealthy, and although he has lived well and enjoyed his money, he became committed to giving back to central Iowa. This notion led to his generous giving and fundraising efforts, making central Iowa a better place to live and work.

Bill Knapp rose from poor rural beginnings to become one of Des Moines's most prominent business figures and philanthropists. His accomplishments were anything but likely, and for many he personified the self-made man. He ascended from rags to riches, to borrow a phrase often associated with nineteenth-century author Horatio Alger, through patience and grit, hard work, and vision. These qualities, along with his "fierce competitiveness and the fear of falling back into poverty," propelled Bill forward.[1]

Other traits were important as well. Although not well educated, Bill possesses a raw intelligence that often makes him the smartest person in any given room. Roger Brooks, the former CEO of Central Life Assurance (now part of Athene USA), once likened Bill "to a chess player several moves ahead of most people." Such moves often included his propensity for envisioning the directions of suburban and commercial growth and buying land ahead of development. Likewise, he had the ability to "push ideas into reality by bringing people together and negotiating and closing deals."[2]

Born in 1926, Bill was raised on a struggling family farm just outside of Allerton, a small town in Wayne County a hundred miles south of Des Moines, amid the deep agricultural depression of the 1920s and 1930s. Here he learned the virtue of hard work, but he also learned that such efforts on the farm did not necessarily result in commensurate financial rewards. Farmers, the youngster understood, had little control over their own destiny; they were always at the mercy of the weather, the fluctuations of the commodity markets, and interest rates.

Bill had no career in mind when he graduated from high school in 1944, but he longed to determine his own future and knew he did not want to farm. That summer, he enlisted in the U.S. Navy and became a pilot for a Landing Craft Vehicle Personnel used to transport Marines and equipment to beachhead invasions. He was assigned to the USS *Catron*, an attack transport, and the following spring he saw action in the Pacific, ferrying troops back and forth at the Battle of Okinawa. He returned from the war in 1946, married his high school sweetheart, Irene Hill, and began the first of several short-term jobs as he searched for something that promised economic independence and keep him off the farm.

He started cleaning equipment at the Allerton Co-op Dairy but was soon ready to move on. Bill then borrowed money through the GI Bill and bought a building in his hometown, where he and Irene started the I & B Café (using the initials of their first names). The restaurant afforded him the chance to shape his own destiny and, as he explains, he "was not subject to someone else's agenda." Business was good and the restaurant enjoyed a steady flow of customers, but because it was open seven days a week, the Knapps had to work all the time. After six months, the couple leased the business and moved to Des Moines in search of something else.[3]

Bill worked a couple of manual labor jobs in the capital city before returning to Allerton, where he tried a stint at his father's sale barn. None of these suited him, and Irene suggested that he again take advantage of the GI Bill and attend the American Institute of Business, a vocational school in Des Moines that offered business courses and could prepare him for a more promising career. Bill agreed, took a yearlong certificate program, and landed a bookkeeping job in 1949. It was a step up from his previous jobs, but the work bored him.

Then a serendipitous moment led Bill to his calling. The couple who rented the Knapps' building and café in Allerton tired of the business that year and did not renew their lease. When Bill and Irene could not find another tenant, they put the building up for sale, listing it with W. K. Brewer, a Des Moines real estate agent. Brewer found a potential buyer, but he could not show the property and asked Bill if he could do it. Bill agreed, showed the Allerton property, and negotiated a deal. He was annoyed when Brewer still received the commission, even though he had made the sale. But a light bulb had gone off in his head. "Hell, I can sell real estate," he remembers thinking.[4]

That was exactly what he did. He talked to Brewer about getting into the business, and the broker sent him to see another real estate agent, Ed Northrup. Northrup hired him in late 1949 and mentored the young man in the art of selling properties. Bill soon obtained his real estate license and enjoyed immediate success selling homes. He loved everything about the business: dealing with clients, negotiating deals, and having the independence that the work afforded him. He also appreciated the commission system, which rewarded his efforts. Bill knew instantly that he had found his niche, recalling, "It was not drudgery, like the earlier jobs I'd held; it never really seemed like work." After about eight months, he moved on to Hollis and Company, a larger real estate agency in downtown Des Moines.[5]

Bill's timing could not have been better. His entry into the business coincided with the post–World War II economic expansion fueled by the baby boom and a huge demand for housing. Des Moines and central Iowa participated in this postwar growth and prosperity, and as one of

Hollis's most aggressive agents, Bill quickly became the company's top salesperson. He bought the agency in 1952 and renamed it Iowa Realty. Bill hired ambitious young men like himself—most important were Kenny Grandquist and then Paul Knapp, his younger brother—and Iowa Realty rapidly became the leading real estate firm in the city. With good people selling properties and soon managing the operation, Bill spent more and more time promoting the firm and meeting and talking with bankers, builders, land developers, and others involved in real estate.

His activity as well as the success of Iowa Realty quickly captured people's attention. William Cotton, a local banker, advised, "Keep an eye on Bill Knapp; that young man is going places," while Lew Clarkson, a longtime area real estate agent, noted, "Bill was always busy." His many hours talking with those in and around the business coupled with his frequent drives around the city gave him a sense of the directions the real estate market was heading. For Clarkson, that became Bill's unique talent; he could gauge where development would take place and use that knowledge to buy land ahead of the expansion. "He had the gift and the guts," Clarkson observed. Competitor Joe Kirk Sr. thought that Bill "saw opportunities others didn't and acted on them."[6]

Bankrolled with profits from Iowa Realty's sale of homes, Bill moved into land development, initially with friend, partner, and builder John Grubb and then on his own. Buying undeveloped land on the outskirts of the city at farm prices, he began opening residential subdivisions, selling the lots at much higher development prices.[7]

Partnered with Grubb, Bill opened the 1960s with two important deals. He negotiated with Hy-Vee Food Stores, a company that was interested in breaking into the Des Moines market. In 1961, he built two markets for the firm on land he and Grubb owned in the city and then leased the facilities to the growing chain. These were the first of a number of lucrative deals Bill would cut with Hy-Vee over his career.

Shortly thereafter, he hammered out his biggest deal to date: he and Grubb bought 275 acres of the Meredith estate, located north of the Beaverdale neighborhood outside the city limits, for $1 million. Many in the business considered the purchase a huge mistake. Ultimately, however, the development proved to be a huge success, but it took longer than Bill had expected. After its first subdivision opened in the mid-1960s, the project stalled, and it was not until the early 1980s that the final lots were sold. Nonetheless, the achievement prompted Grubb's son, John W. Grubb, to comment on Bill's knack of seeing the potential in undeveloped land that others did not: "He had a better crystal ball than the rest of us."[8]

This ability led him into commercial projects as well. After sections of the Interstate 80–Interstate 35 highway system through Des Moines were completed in 1960, Bill saw that the city could become a hub for interstate trucking, which would require warehouses. He bought land at the interchange of these highways for an industrial park. Interstate Acres opened in 1966, and over the next few years it became an important site for commercial and industrial development. Bill followed these successes with rewarding forays into the hotel and restaurant business as well as continued involvement in new residential subdivisions and commercial developments.

In the late 1970s, Bill's interest turned to downtown Des Moines, where trucking magnate John Ruan and others had kicked off a renaissance earlier in the decade. Here again, Bill saw something that colleagues and rivals had missed when he bought the dilapidated Hotel Savery. He poured millions into its restoration, making the hotel and Guido's, its illustrious restaurant, the most fashionable spot in town. At the same time, Bill joined with other business figures in the Des Moines Development Corporation, a nonprofit tied to the Greater Des Moines Chamber of Commerce, to encourage economic development in the downtown area.

Actually, he became the nonprofit's biggest proponent of rebuilding downtown Des Moines. Fred Weitz, the former CEO of the Weitz Company, remembered Bill as the organization's key figure: "Bill understood people, he understood deals, and he got things done." Bill orchestrated the acquisition of the run-down properties just west of the then new Nollen Plaza (now Cowles Commons) and then secured major tenants for the eight-story building (Capital Square) to ensure that it was erected. He then played a prominent role in several other new structures downtown in the 1980s. Most significant was the Plaza, the city's first luxury high-rise condominiums, located just south and east of the Civic Center of Greater Des Moines.[9]

Meanwhile, the deep economic recession that began in the late 1970s brought rising unemployment and interest rates, which meant tough times for the real estate business. Many firms across the nation downsized, merged, or went out of business. As the number of real estate companies in Des Moines fell sharply in the early 1980s, Bill's chief rival, Gene Stanbrough, the owner of Stanbrough/Better Homes and Gardens Real Estate, thought survival in the difficult market required growth and expansion. He thus created First Group in 1983, buying two smaller competitors and adding a bank, an insurance operation, a property management company, and a construction business under one umbrella.[10]

Bill was also looking to strengthen Iowa Realty's position and found a ready partner in Roger Brooks, the head of Des Moines–based Central Life Assurance. Central Life bought 80 percent of Iowa Realty in 1984, but Bill and his management team were given a free hand to run the operation as they saw fit. Bill believed that with access to Central Life's capital, he could make more money by owning 20 percent of the company than he could when he had controlled all of it.

He was right. With Central Life providing financing at below market rates, Bill began several big subdivisions, which provided the firm with many new homes to sell. Iowa Realty's sales volume more than doubled over the next three years, rising from $169 million in 1985 to $341 million in 1988.[11]

Late that year, Brooks opened negotiations with Bill to buy the rest of Iowa Realty. The deal closed the following spring, with Central Life buying the outstanding shares of the firm for $7.99 million, 20 percent more than it had paid for the first 80 percent of the company five years earlier. As before, Bill and Iowa Realty's top managers signed contracts to stay in place for the next several years.

With Bill out negotiating deals and his brother, Paul, looking toward retirement, Bill's two nephews, Mike Knapp and his brother Bill

Knapp II, moved up through the management ranks of Iowa Realty; undoubtedly, they were the heirs apparent. In 1991, Mike was named senior vice president of Iowa Realty's brokerage business; he would go on to replace his father, Paul, as the company's chairman and CEO. Bill II advanced to senior vice president of operations, which included property management and development.

The following year, Bill created Knapp Properties to manage his vast property holdings, which had been overseen by Iowa Realty before Central Life bought the rest of the company. Bill headed the operation as chairman, Bill II was vice chairman, and the two soon hired private practice attorney Gerry Neugent, who for years had done a great deal of Iowa Realty's legal work, as the company's president and CEO. Through Knapp Properties, Bill continued wheeling and dealing. His greatest success came in 2004, when he sold 136 acres just south of Jordan Creek Town Center to Wells Fargo and then another 76 acres to develop and build the Galleria shopping area just to the east. He sold the first parcel for more than a hundred times what he had paid for it, while the second piece of ground sold for more than three hundred times the purchase price.

Bill also grew active in Democratic politics. His interest started in 1962 when he became acquainted with then gubernatorial candidate Harold Hughes, who went on to serve as governor of Iowa from 1963 to 1969 and then as U.S. senator from 1970 to 1975. His relationship with Hughes connected Bill with many other prominent Iowa Democrats, and over time Bill became one of the state party's leading donors and most influential power brokers.

By the 1990s, several changes had taken place. Bill II and Gerry Neugent took over the day-to-day operations of Knapp Properties. At the same time, Bill's twenty-year relationship with businesswoman Connie Wimer, which had broken up his forty-year marriage to Irene the previous decade, came to an end. Soon, however, sixty-six-year-old Bill began seeing forty-one-year-old Susan Terry. The friendship quickly turned romantic, and the two moved in together in 1995. They married three years later, and despite the age difference, it was clear that the two were well suited to each other.

The other change involved Bill's focus. Although he remained active in business and was always looking for opportunities, he devoted more of his time to philanthropic endeavors. Years earlier, progressive politician Harold Hughes had pointed him in that direction, but it was friend David Kruidenier, the former publisher of the *Des Moines Register* and *Tribune*, who inspired Bill to open his wallet and really start giving back to the community. He took this up with the same zeal and enthusiasm he brought to real estate. Besides giving millions of his own, Bill was a tireless advocate for his favorite charitable organizations and nonprofits, cajoling friends and colleagues to ante up as well. Important institutions that benefited from his support and largesse included, for instance, Des Moines's Tiny Tots Childcare Center, the Homes of Oakridge, Drake University, Planned Parenthood, the development of Gray's Lake Park, the Iowa State Fair, the Iowa Veterans Cemetery, Central Iowa Honor Flight, Meals from the Heartland, and Iowa Methodist Medical Center (now part of Unity Point Health).

Until very recently, Bill has always concentrated on the present. When his latest deal was concluded, whether it be buying or selling land, opening a major development, or making a large donation, he moved on. He never dwelled on the past but instead went on to the next project. However, now in his early nineties, Bill has started looking back, taking measure of his life. He clearly made much of his own success, certainly as much as any self-made person, and he is rightly proud of his accomplishments.

Along the way, Bill's experience has taught him important business lessons that have guided him over his seventy-plus years in the world of real estate. But he also understands that no one is truly self-made. He had the good fortune of knowing and then working with key people who helped him at critical junctures in his career.

What follows is not a full-fledged biography of Bill; that can be found in my 2013 *The Real Deal: The Life of Bill Knapp*. Instead, this volume focuses on the making of the man by exploring two life-defining themes. Part One examines and analyzes the lessons Bill learned and traces the ways they guided him throughout his career. Part Two identifies and describes the significant individuals and one company who were indispensable to Bill's success.

PART ONE

Bill Knapp's Top 10 Business Tenets

Like other successful people, Bill Knapp tended to be a quick study and learned a variety of lessons on the job. He picked up some almost immediately, while others took longer to embrace. Experience taught Bill what worked, and these ideas grew into the basic tenets that guided the way he operated, whether he was negotiating deals, overseeing Iowa Realty and then Knapp Properties, or amassing an empire of hundreds of properties and thousands of acres in central Iowa.

"DO WHAT YOU LIKE, AND IT WILL NEVER BE WORK"

Chapter One

Develop a passion rather than follow one. That was what Bill did when he fell into the real estate business. Up to that time, his main reason for taking jobs was to avoid returning to the farm. But becoming a real estate agent opened a whole new world for him. It played to his strengths of talking with people and reading them. He cultivated these gifts and soon was selling many homes. It was here that he honed his negotiating skills, and making deals with builders, bankers, developers, and others would soon become his stock in trade. There were, of course, aspects of the real estate business that he did not enjoy and where he did not excel, but he found ways to avoid these and focus on what he did best.

Bill's talent for and then interest in the business became evident almost immediately. Shortly after hiring him in 1950, agency owner Byron Hollis said that Bill "was the most outstanding recruit ever to come onto the Des Moines real estate street. He had rapport with prospects. He had the touch, the ability to get the confidence of investors . . . and keep them happy."[1]

Bill's zeal for the business, his skills, and his willingness to put in long hours rapidly made him Hollis's leading salesman. A couple of years later, Bill bought the agency, and Iowa Realty was born.

Roger Cleven, one of Iowa Realty's agents, said of his boss in the early 1950s, "Bill was totally committed to business." Cleven's assessment was right on target. Bill loved what he was doing, and his life revolved around real estate. He was constantly thinking about or working on the next deal, the next land development, or the next way to expand the company, and the barrier between work and home or business and leisure ceased to exist for him. He truly did eat, sleep, and breathe real estate.[2]

His business associates and friends were regularly one and the same. Kenny Grandquist, who was Bill's most important early hire, quickly became Iowa Realty's top salesperson and then sales manager. He also became Bill's best friend. In fact, Grandquist and his wife, Evelyn, became neighbors to Bill and Irene in 1953 and then in 1958, when the two couples built homes next door to each other in the Beaverdale neighborhood, north and west of downtown. Bill and Grandquist would repeat this again in 1965, building new homes a few blocks to the northwest. The couples and their growing families vacationed together as well, first at a Knapp-owned cottage in Clear Lake, a hundred miles north of Des Moines, and later in Florida.[3]

Builder John Grubb and his family often joined them on these vacations. Sometimes the vacationing group included Bill's brother, Paul—who had joined Iowa Realty in the mid-1950s—and his family as well. Originally, they all went to Miami before switching to Florida's gulf side and going to Naples and later Siesta Key, a barrier island just east of Sarasota. There Bill and Irene as well as the Grandquists and the Grubbs all bought condominiums in the same building, and there, soaking up the winter sun, Bill's conversations were normally about the real estate business.[4]

By the 1980s, Bill began spending more of the winter in Florida, but he remained in close contact with his managers in Des Moines and worked on central Iowa deals over the phone. He also briefly maintained a real estate office in Naples to, as he put it, "stay involved when I was away from home." Clearly, Bill could not set business aside; he needed to be in the middle of the action.[5]

Bill did enjoy some pastimes outside of business. He became a firm believer in the benefits of physical fitness, for example, and exercised religiously, but he connected that interest with his business as well. He built a workout room in Iowa Realty's Beaver Avenue office basement and later added a massage table, where he got massages after his workouts, all without leaving the office. Bill had taken up tennis in the late 1950s, but as with his vacations, he played with Grandquist, Paul, and others from Iowa Realty. Other than calling out the score, talk on the court usually revolved around business.[6]

Over the course of his life, Bill's friends and activities changed somewhat, but business remained at the center of all he did. In his seventies he began playing golf, a sport he had long detested because a round often took up to five hours, time better spent, he thought, selling homes and making money. But he came to realize that deals could be made on the golf course, and sure enough, once he started golfing, he could frequently be found doing business between holes.[7]

He also grew fond of hunting turkey or deer in the fall, usually with retired cable executive Jim Cownie, a good friend and business partner. But even here, Cownie recalled, in the most implausible of places, Bill could not miss an opportunity to close a transaction. Once, when he and Bill were in the woods up in their tree stands waiting to spot a deer, Cownie heard Bill talking. He looked over and saw his friend on his cell phone, hammering out a deal.[8]

Likewise, Bill found that social gatherings proved fertile ground for conducting business. Every year Bill and Susan, his second wife, threw a lavish party in early December. Here leading figures in central Iowa business, cultural, political, and philanthropic circles gathered for the opening of the holiday season. And here Bill talked deals. As his longtime associate Gerry Neugent was leaving the 2010 party, he lightheartedly asked Bill how many deals he had closed that evening. "Only one," Bill replied. They laughed as Neugent headed out.[9]

But that was Bill Knapp. Business was his life and his life was business. He was well aware of his singular focus, once joking with journalist, businessman, and majority owner of the Iowa Cubs Michael Gartner that he had been so sick while recovering from complications after knee surgery that he did not even think about real estate. That was a rare occurrence indeed. Bill loved being engaged and involved in negotiating deals, and once he found he could do this for a living, he never experienced the drudgery of work again.[10]

"YOU CAN'T DO IT ALL BY YOURSELF"

Chapter Two

Your success depends on others. Hire talented people, compensate them well, and show them appreciation. "Give people who helped you get where you are credit, and never lose important associates because of money."[1]

One afternoon in 1950, shortly after Bill and Irene had purchased their first home, the young real estate agent was painting their new house. While working up on a ladder, Bill received several phone calls about pending real estate deals. Each time that he climbed down and took the call, he became more and more frustrated. The painting, he thought, was interrupting what he should be doing—selling homes—and he imagined how many more deals he could be closing if he were not tied up working around the house. When yet another call came in, his anger boiled over, and he yelled to Irene, "Let's hire [the painting] done!" From that point on, Bill's modus operandi was to hire others to do household chores, freeing him up to focus on real estate deals.[2]

More significant, however, this also became an essential component of Bill's success at Iowa Realty. When he acquired the company, he understood that it was critical to have a team of energetic, aggressive agents working for him. The core group stayed with him after he took over, and he added solid salespeople to his workforce. But he knew his shortcomings and realized that he did not have the skills or the desire to administer the operation. "I'm glad I made enough money to hire people smarter than I to do the things I couldn't do or didn't want to do."[3]

Specifically, Bill needed managers who could oversee people. He found his first key manager in Kenny Grandquist. This freed Bill up to do deals and search for new opportunities. Bill's brother, Paul, would succeed Grandquist in this position in the mid-1970s. As the next generation moved up the company's management ladder, Paul's son Mike moved into the role.

Likewise, Bill was never interested in the nitty-gritty, as he called it; he needed people to follow up on the details once he had closed a deal. His good friend and Des Moines attorney Bill Wimer was the first to do this from the late 1950s up to the mid-1980s, when Paul Knapp's middle son, Bill Knapp II, who had become Iowa Realty's in-house counsel, took over the job.[4]

Putting together a solid team was critical, but Bill also knew that retaining those people was equally important. To that end, he learned that compensating his employees well and showing them appreciation went a long way. His former boss Byron Hollis had been a poor money manager and was often unable to pay his agents their full commissions, leading many to leave the operation. Bill, in fact, had acquired the Hollis agency in lieu of $8,000 in back commissions he was owed.[5]

Once he took over the company, Bill was careful to pay his agents their full commissions immediately after home sales closed. He also began offering incentives to recognize top performers and increase sales. When agents met Iowa Realty's goals, Bill took them and their spouses out for steak dinners. In one especially good year, he took top salesmen and their wives on a weekend trip to Chicago. Such programs helped Iowa Realty keep talented agents, while those who did not meet sales expectations did not remain with the company long.[6]

Nonetheless, top agents sometimes left Iowa Realty to start their own business or work for a competitor. Fortunately, these losses were usually only temporary setbacks, but they made Bill realize that he could not afford to lose Kenny Grandquist. He reasoned that part ownership in the company would be a powerful incentive to stay. From the late 1950s into the early 1960s, therefore, he gave Iowa Realty stock to Grandquist and then to his brother. Grandquist ended up with a 30 percent stake in the company, while Paul had 10 percent.[7]

But Bill's unwillingness to provide such inducements on a wider basis cost him dearly in the mid-1960s. Ed Cooper, who oversaw the company's high-volume office on Des Moines's south side, thought he deserved a percentage of the sales for managing the office. When Bill refused, Cooper and the other two agents in the office left to start their own business.

Bill not only lost three leading salespeople, he also had to close the south side office because no one else at Iowa Realty had experience selling in this section of the city.[8]

After this exodus, Bill did not want to lose any other key people over compensation issues. By the early 1970s, therefore, he became more proactive about retention and created a profit-sharing program for corporate staff. He stepped up this effort several years later by adding a stock ownership plan for important employees. In 1984, the company extended the profit-sharing plan to all its agents, making it one of the first real estate firms to do so.[9]

These efforts paid off. With the right people in place and generous remuneration packages to keep them there, Bill and his team built Iowa Realty and then Knapp Properties into highly successful companies. Today both firms pride themselves on their employee longevity, which is largely due to programs and incentives that Bill established years earlier.[10]

"BUILD RELATIONSHIPS AND KEEP IN TOUCH"

Chapter Three

Business is based on relationships. Creating and then maintaining a network will give you visibility, keep you well informed, and often result in useful ideas, clients, partners, and deals.

Bill always enjoyed visiting with people. When he and Irene owned their Allerton café, he ran the front of the restaurant, where he loved chatting and connecting with customers. Later in real estate, he quickly recognized that schmoozing with others in and around the industry paid dividends. Socializing could yield useful information; even more likely, such mingling could lead to friendships and result in partnerships or deals.

Once Bill had Kenny Grandquist heading up a reliable management structure at Iowa Realty, he stepped up his efforts to develop business and make deals. This meant meeting and building relationships with those familiar with area real estate, land development, finance, urban planning, and the like. He would go to lunch and dinner or have drinks with such people, hoping to leverage these connections into building his business or creating deals.

Bill's independent streak, however, kept him from joining many clubs, service organizations, or trade associations. He understood that their goals might be worthy, but he saw their meetings and gatherings as tedious.

"Other people enjoyed that kind of thing, but I saw it as a waste of time," he recalled. Still, he was a realist, and he knew that membership in some organizations could result in valuable friendships and build his business.[1]

In the 1950s, therefore, Bill joined the Scottish Rite Masons, rose through the ranks, and along with fellow Mason John Grubb, he even joined Des Moines's Za-Ga-Zig Shrine. Ultimately, however, he attended their functions only when necessary. The same went for the Greater Des Moines Board of Realtors, the local affiliate of the National Association of Realtors. While Bill believed the group was important for the industry, he left it to others to run, rarely attended local meetings, and never went to the national convention. This ended temporarily in 1969 when, despite his protests, he was elected president of the central Iowa group.[2]

Even though rubbing elbows with business associates was one of Bill's top priorities, most group activities were not for him, but the Breakfast Club was an exception. Begun in 1962 by Des Moines insurance agent Peter Choconas, the organization met every Tuesday morning, initially at the Hotel Savery. It brought together leaders from various businesses in the city, offering them a place to meet and socialize as well as exchange ideas and do deals. Bill joined the group in 1963, and as he had hoped, the networking opportunities proved valuable. It was here, for example, that he developed a friendship with banker David Miller, which eventually led to Bill's partnership with him to buy the Blue Horizon Motel in Clear Lake. A year later, in 1984, Miller invited Bill into a consortium that bought West Des Moines State Bank (now West Bank).[3]

Besides staying in touch with those in and around the real estate industry, Bill also cultivated friendships with elected or appointed municipal officials. As John Grubb put it, "Bill made friends with people in parts of government that would do him the most good." Even though such relationships did not always pay off, Grubb felt that Bill almost "always got a favorable reception on the Plan and Zoning Commission and the City Council," two bodies critical to the land development business.[4]

When he could not meet with people in person, Bill kept in close touch by telephone. Cecelia "Cee" Gentry, his longtime administrative assistant, referred to the telephone as "his lifeline," recalling that "he kept abreast of things on the phone." It was not at all surprising, therefore, that in the early 1980s Bill was one of the first people in Des Moines to get a mobile phone, and Gentry remembered that it was a "big clunky brick of a thing, and he would always answer it, whether he was at home, on the tennis court, or in his car."[5]

Bill was obsessed with staying connected, and he became especially fond of the ease of using the telephone: "It was quick, and it was easy. I could find out information, get a donation, or close a deal all in a matter of minutes. Then I could hang up, dial another number, and talk to someone else."[6]

Longtime associate Gerry Neugent noted, "Bill has always been great at meeting new people, building relationships, and staying in touch." Early on, Bill had grasped that business was based on connections. "Who you knew," he observed, "was important." He therefore constantly worked at developing and maintaining his network of friends, partners, and business associates, because for Bill they were all one and the same. As accountant Jack Wahlig put it, "Bill was always open for business." The statement captured Bill perfectly. Whether in the office or at home, at a party or out with friends, on the tennis court or later the golf course, in town or on vacation, he was all about putting together the next deal, and his carefully nurtured web of connections made this possible.[7]

"BUY AND HOLD LAND"

Chapter Four

The practice of buying and holding land is not unique to Bill and, in fact, is a relatively common investment scheme. But Bill is a big believer in the strategy and has used it to greater success than most.

"Trial and error," he remembered, as well as his early "observation that real estate appreciated in value over time" led to him to adopt this strategy. This approach contrasted sharply with that of friend and builder John Grubb, a frequent business partner in the late 1950s and early 1960s. Grubb usually focused on the quick profit—often buying land, developing it, and then selling it as rapidly as possible. Bill, however, was much more willing to sit on the land and wait, in Grubb's words, for "later money."[1]

Using his various connections to gather information and spending many hours driving around greater Des Moines, Bill imagined where future bustling subdivisions, retail districts, or commercial parks would be built, and it was there that he quietly bought land. His willingness to wait for a profit proved lucrative in both the Meredith estate deal and that of Interstate Acres. Later, this willingness to wait for land values to rise led him to buy a number of acreages during the farm crisis of the 1980s. Brother Paul remembered, "Bill bought a lot of farmland [early in that decade] because he thought it was at the bottom, and he proved to be right. I've learned that when Bill makes a decision to go along with it, because he has been right on almost everything."[2]

Bill explained his success to a reporter in 1990: "When you've been in the business as long as I have, you kind of have a feeling of where development is going to go." Sometimes, however, waiting was not necessary.[3]

Shortly after Bill bought 570 acres of farmland stretching across western Polk County and eastern Dallas County in 1987, for instance, Iowa Realty announced its $100 million, 400-acre Country Club development situated in the narrow suburb of Clive, sandwiched between West Des Moines and Urbandale. Plans called for hundreds of upscale homes, expensive townhomes, and a 45-acre lake to be created from a Walnut Creek tributary.[4]

Bill's purchase and then Iowa Realty's development plans generated tremendous interest. Other developers followed his lead, buying parcels in the area. Marvin Pomerantz's real estate development company, the Mid-America Group, for instance, acquired 150 acres on the northeastern boundary of Country Club and opened its own luxury residential subdivision, the Woodlands. More important for Bill and Iowa Realty was the incredible reception from the public. Months before construction began, the company had a waiting list of people wanting to buy lakeside lots, and when the first plat opened in July 1988, the seventy lots sold out in a week. The development ultimately became Iowa Realty's largest and most successful.[5]

Meanwhile, the other 170 acres Bill had purchased south and east of Country Club were prepared for commercial use. Bill's connections brought him two early and significant tenants, and from there the development took off. Iowa Methodist Medical Center (now part of Unity Point Health), a longtime partner of Bill's, bought 20 acres in the development, soon to be named West Lakes Business Park, in spring 1988, and several months later bought another 40 acres. Here Iowa Methodist would construct several buildings that would become Lakeview Medical Park. Meanwhile Hy-Vee, another of Bill's long-standing corporate partners, bought 21 acres in the development for its new headquarters. With two major tenants nailed down, Bill then partnered with Farm Bureau Life Insurance Company, which owned an adjacent 100-acre tract, and expanded the business park. He then landed Kirke–Van Orsdel, a Des Moines–based insurance company, which announced plans to build a $20 million facility in 1991.[6]

The rapid successes at Country Club and West Lakes were not the rule, however, and Bill's willingness to wait for "later money" paid off repeatedly. After buying 364 acres in Booneville, eighteen miles west of downtown Des Moines, in 1986, he immediately began preparing the property for an upscale residential development. Situated on a bluff over the Raccoon River Valley, the land had been owned by Crawford Hubbell, who had had it rezoned for residential use. After he started to put in roads and water lines, infrastructure work stopped when Hubbell went bankrupt in the mid-1980s. Once the land was Bill's, he and his team overhauled the luxury subdivision plans to include a swimming pool, tennis courts, a driving range, a putting green, and a picnic area. It was renamed Napa Valley, a reference to the elegant wine-growing region in California and a play on Knapp's name. Accordingly, streets were named in honor of wines—Burgundy Circle, Chardonnay Point, Champagne Road, and Vintage Point—and a small vineyard was planted on the grounds.[7]

Napa Valley opened a little over a year after the land's purchase, but because of the high price of the oversized lots and because of the distance from Des Moines, Bill did not expect to sell more than 12 of the 155 lots per year. He was surprised when sales were initially brisk—50 lots sold in a little over two years. However, sales slowed for several years before picking up again in the mid-1990s as metro residential developments continued pushing westward toward Booneville.[8]

Other examples of Bill finding great success buying and holding land abound, but two are especially noteworthy. In the 1980s, he bought 570 wooded acres in Polk City, a small town sixteen miles north of Des Moines. Years later, in 2000, Minneapolis-based Enebak Construction and its subsidiary, Traditions Golf, approached Bill and Knapp Properties about building an Arnold Palmer–designed golf course and residential community in greater Des Moines. They formed a partnership, and after plans to develop the project on land Bill owned above the Raccoon River in eastern Dallas County fell through, the group chose to lay out the development on the land Bill had in Polk City near Big Creek Reservoir. The community was to have six hundred homes and townhomes around the eighteen-hole golf course. When construction began, there was a waiting list to purchase home lots, and the golf course opened in 2003. Individuals and developers snapped up lots until the economic downturn in 2007, but sales resumed several years later, and by 2012 the original subdivision was sold out. It took nearly three decades, but Bill reaped large profits from his earlier Polk City land acquisition.[9]

The most spectacular success of Bill's buy and hold strategy took place in West Des Moines. In 1987, he bought the 375-acre Staples farm in what was then unincorporated eastern Dallas County for $1,100 per acre and waited for development to push westward. And it did: area land prices experienced a huge jump in 2002, when General Growth Properties paid $81,000 per acre for 216 acres just north of the Staples farm to build Jordan Creek Town Center. At about the same time, West Des Moines–based Wells Fargo Home Mortgage began looking to expand. Bill urged his neighbor and friend Mark Oman, the head of the bank's home mortgage division, to move its headquarters to a portion of the Staples farm. While Bill's relationship with Oman certainly did not hurt, the division president was not involved in picking the location for the company's new facility.[10]

While Wells Fargo contemplated various sites in greater Des Moines, Bill lobbied company officials about the advantages of locating its new facility on his land south of the rising shopping center. Negotiations continued until Bill sold the firm 136 acres of the farm at an incredible $121,000 per acre. Shortly thereafter, Knapp Properties joined with Ron Daniels's Buyers Realty in a development group and then sold the consortium 73 acres of the remaining Staples farmland to the east of the Wells Fargo site at $300,000 per acre. There they built the Galleria shopping center, which would soon include a Walmart Supercenter, TJ Maxx, OfficeMax, Trader Joe's, and Pier One Imports.[11]

Such remarkable success led Bill Knapp II to say, "We've had some great luck." Then he joked, "If you buy enough land, eventually a highway or sewer is going to be built." Bill added, "You can't guess right on all your land purchases. We've made mistakes and bought land that lost money or didn't make money, but those usually go unnoticed." Still, Bill was right much more often than he was wrong in his purchases, and he was renowned for his vision and foresight in buying and holding land, eventually turning fields or woods into residential neighborhoods, retail districts, and office or commercial space.[12]

"DON'T DWELL ON THE PAST; IF YOU DO, YOU LOSE FOCUS ON THE PRESENT"

Chapter Five

Pay attention to the immediate task. Your successes as well as your mistakes are in the past; learn from both, but concentrate on the present. Bill had the uncanny ability to be in the moment. "He was always hyperfocused on the current deal he was working on, but once it was done, he didn't look back," recalls Gerry Neugent, and he was off pursuing a new project.[1]

Of course, Bill appreciated accolades, reveled in recognition, and savored successes. But after pausing to enjoy these moments, he moved on. When a colleague mentioned an advantageous transaction Bill had just negotiated, he responded, "That was last year's bonus," and it was clear that he was already thinking about the next deal.[2]

He likewise despised losing and making mistakes. Two notable blunders were costly, but just like his successes, he never dwelled on these or any other failures. The first involved land Bill had originally purchased in the early 1970s for $1,475 per acre, which eventually became part of West Lakes Business Park. At the end of the decade, he transferred the land to Kenny Grandquist as part of the settlement dissolving their partnership. At the time, it was valued at $607,500 or about $6,400 per acre. Years later, however, in 1991, he repurchased the 95-acre parcel, then owned jointly by Hubbell Realty and the Allied Group, Incorporated, paying the hefty market price of $4 million.[3]

Bill later could laugh about the transactions: "I bought it low, sold it low edge, and bought it back high." But when he was asked if he regretted these deals, he replied instantly, "No, I never look back. I never second-guess a decision I've made. If I'd kept the land, then I wouldn't have been able to buy other things." The answer was vintage Bill: even before the ink had dried on the contract, he had moved past the purchase and was surveying the landscape for other investment possibilities. Spending time mulling over done deals might mean he would miss a new opportunity.[4]

One such prospect appeared in the late 1980s, when Bill and Iowa Realty collaborated with developer Denny Elwell in a fifty-fifty partnership to purchase more than seven hundred acres in Ankeny, a sleepy suburb twelve miles north of Des Moines. Both were bullish on the potential for the city's growth, and Bill told a *Des Moines Register* reporter, "Ankeny is coming to life. I feel the time is right here. It's Ankeny's day in the sun." They planned to transform their ground into commercial parks and residential neighborhoods, which they estimated would bring in $100 million in new construction in five to eight years.[5]

Once the first residential subdivision was ready, lots were sold to builders, who then listed their newly constructed homes with Iowa Realty. During a meeting, Elwell said that since he was an equal partner with Bill and Iowa Realty, he deserved half the commission made from each home sale. Bill and his brother, Paul, balked at the notion, arguing that home sales were an entirely different business and that the builders did not have to list their houses with Iowa Realty. Elwell persisted, however, saying that he did not know if he could work with someone who was unwilling to partner all the way. At that point, Bill suggested that it might be best for Elwell to buy him out or vice versa. Elwell agreed and purchased Bill and Iowa Realty's half interest.[6]

However, just as Bill had told a *Register* reporter, Ankeny was ready to take off, and the property in question soared in value. The commercial and residential developments carved out of the land once shared in the partnership proved a huge success for Elwell, and in a rare admission

Bill says that selling his interest "had been a hell of a mistake." Still, he wonders, "What did we do with the money we got from the sale? Did we make more money than we could have staying with Denny?" As always, Bill was then off searching for the next deal.[7]

"CLOSE DEALS QUICKLY, AND AIM FOR A WIN-WIN"

Chapter Six

Timelines for deals are short; transactions have expiration dates. "If a deal is going to happen," Bill mused, "it will happen fast. Get in and get it done, or it will blow up." He then added one of his favorite quips, "Nothing gets better with time than wine, and I'm not so sure about wine."[1]

Real estate rival Gene Stanbrough explained Bill's prowess doing deals: "He had a nose for a deal and wasn't afraid to move on it. He could smell a good one, and he could smell a bad one. This gave him a huge edge. Not only was he involved in areas the rest of us weren't, he was really good at making great deals."[2]

Bill had come a long way from his childhood negotiating skills. According to family lore, during the Great Depression Bill and brother Paul were sent to a neighbor's farm to buy a rooster. Their father had told them they could pay up to 60 cents for the fowl. After a short conversation, the farmer said he would sell them the bird for 25 cents. "Oh, no," Bill replied emphatically, "we will go as high as 50 or 60 cents!"[3]

Key to any deal, Bill believes, is knowing when to act. "Sometimes, a property gets bought out from under you unless you move fast." This happened to Bill in 1986. Pat Greene, one of Iowa Realty's leading commercial agents, told Bill that the once popular Rusty Scupper restaurant, which had closed two years earlier, was up for sale. It was located in Des Moines on Grand Avenue three blocks west of Terrace Hill. Bill was interested and told Bill II to look into it and set up an appointment with the owner, but he was busy following up on other deals and did not get to it. The two finally drove to see the property and liked it, and Bill told Bill II to write up an offer. While they were there, Dan Rupprecht, the president of R & R Investors (now R&R Realty Group), drove by and saw them. He was interested in the property as well, especially because he had just completed an office building next door and was considering building a companion structure if he could get the Rusty Scupper lot.[4]

When Rupprecht saw Bill and Bill II, he realized that he was not the only one interested in the restaurant site, and he immediately drove to eastern Iowa to see the owner and submitted an offer on the building. When Bill learned that his offer was too late, he razzed Bill II about not acting fast enough and missing the boat. Over the next few years, Bill would nudge Bill II into action by saying, "Remember the Rusty Scupper."[5]

When deals get to the negotiation stage, Bill still holds to his notion of acting quickly. "If talks drag out, people start to raise questions and see all kinds of problems. Buyer's or seller's remorse creeps in. Any deal that takes too long isn't going to happen." But it is equally important to think long-term. Bill explains, "You can make ten good deals, but if you make one bad deal and cheat someone, it negates the other ten because that is the one people remember."[6]

One deal that gnawed at him was with Des Moines builder Reed Davidson. In 1979, Iowa Realty had taken out an option on Davidson's seventy-two-unit Camelot West Apartments in West Des Moines, with plans to convert the complex to condominiums. Iowa Realty's Midland Builders began painting and carpeting the common areas, but two issues soon halted the project. Bill II discovered that the apartments had been built over a sewer easement, which would complicate the conversion, and rising interest rates dampened the market for condominiums. Given these factors, Bill decided not to exercise the option to buy the property and walked away. Davidson was angry, and although Bill was well within his legal rights, he felt bad about backing out.[7]

He therefore looked for a new deal he could cut with Davidson, one they would each benefit from. He soon found it in 1980, when he bought the contractor's recently completed Des Moines apartment building, known by its address of 4323 Grand, and converted the units to condominiums. Three years later, with the economy rebounding and while being fully aware of the sewer issue, Bill resurrected the Camelot West deal with Davidson. He paid more for the complex than he would have in 1979, but he and the builder were pleased with the transaction, and as Bill had originally planned, he converted the apartments to condominiums.[8]

These deals with Davidson reflected another aspect that Bill considered when doing deals. Although he loved to win, he normally tamped down his competitive spirit in favor of win-win outcomes. "You've got to leave room for the other person to make money," he noted, "and you've got to deal honestly and forthrightly, or people don't want to deal with you." But there was also a selfish angle to this: he had learned that such transactions frequently led to future and sometimes even bigger deals with the same people. And in typical Bill fashion, he explains this thinking with an old adage, "You can shear a sheep many times, but you can only skin him once."[9]

"DON'T HOLD GRUDGES"

Chapter Seven

Never let perceived injustices get in the way of maintaining relationships. There may be occasions to do deals with those who you believe previously wronged you. Do not close doors to opportunities because of past antagonisms.

Maybe it was because Bill was so focused on the present, but he typically was able to work with people even after having had problems with them earlier. There were two instances, however, where it took Bill a long time to renew relationships that had been badly damaged by deep animosities.

The first involved Kenny Grandquist, his longtime close friend and key colleague at Iowa Realty. After having spent over twenty years with Bill at Iowa Realty, Grandquist quit in 1977 because he thought he was being pushed aside in favor of Paul Knapp. He then established his own firm, Universal Realty.

Bill was angry when Grandquist left and started a rival company, but the situation was worsened by the 30 percent stake he held in Iowa Realty as well as the money he had in its profit-sharing plan. He wanted to cash out, but Bill dragged his feet, not wanting to fund a competitor. The feud grew nastier when Grandquist sued Iowa Realty for his portion of the profit-sharing plan, but a settlement was finally reached in 1979. Grandquist received a generous payment to leave Universal Realty and sign a noncompete clause stating that he would stay out of the central Iowa real estate business for five years; he also received his $250,000 from the profit-sharing plan and nearly $4 million worth of properties for his Iowa Realty stock.[1]

Over the next few years, Bill edged toward repairing the damaged friendship. Grandquist had been working on building a horse track and establishing pari-mutuel racing in central Iowa. He had obtained the required racing license, gained the city of Altoona's approval for a track, and put together a finance package, which involved issuing $40 million in revenue bonds. But the project stalled when the bonds did not sell, and it was Bill who stepped forward in spring 1986 to help his old friend. He became the first prominent member of the Des Moines business community to provide public support for Grandquist's track, pledging to invest $100,000 in the project. Unfortunately for Grandquist, this was too little too late; he withdrew his proposal and his license went to former city manager Richard Wilkey, who would make Grandquist's dream come true by overseeing the development and opening of Prairie Meadows Racetrack in 1989.[2]

Meanwhile, Bill and Grandquist returned to their old ways, and when Grandquist built a mansion in Bill's Napa Valley in the late 1980s, Bill soon followed, erecting an identical home next door to his former partner. The two also resumed doing deals together. In the early 1990s, for instance, Bill and his brother, Paul, along with Grandquist and his brother, John, who had also worked at Iowa Realty heading up its home-building division, bought ten acres on the north side of Fuller Road (now Mills Civic Parkway) across from the Glen Oaks community, then under development. Several years later, they sold the land to a group headed by businessman Gary Kirke, and the parcel would later become the western portion of West Glen Town Center, a residential, entertainment, and shopping district.[3]

Even before Bill's friendship with Grandquist initially soured, he had had a falling-out with entrepreneur and real estate developer Marvin

Pomerantz. Business had brought Bill and Pomerantz together in the late 1960s, and the two became fast friends. In the early 1970s, Bill was considering purchasing a piece of land in Urbandale and took Pomerantz to see it. Pomerantz liked the parcel as well, and he suggested that he buy and develop it as a residential subdivision and give Bill and Iowa Realty exclusive rights to sell all its lots and homes. Bill agreed, and Pomerantz closed on the land and began improving the property, bounded by Meredith Drive to the north, Seventy-Fifth Street to the east, Aurora Avenue to the south, and Eighty-Sixth Street to the west.[4]

But when it came time to start marketing the lots in the development, known as Parkview, Pomerantz did not recall their agreement the way Bill did, and he did not use Iowa Realty to sell home sites. Bill was furious and believed that Pomerantz had reneged on their deal. He made his views clear one day as the two rode the Ruan Center elevator down from the Des Moines Club (now the Des Moines Embassy Club). Then the two stopped speaking.[5]

The situation grew even worse a year or two later over a West Des Moines land deal. Pomerantz had purchased land from the Meredith Corporation south of Westown Parkway in the late 1970s, where he would soon begin construction of the multibuilding Regency West Business Park. Shortly after this acquisition, Bill convinced friend and business leader John Ruan to buy a large piece of land on the north side of Westown Parkway, across from the Pomerantz parcel. Ruan planned on purchasing the land, which would mean a big commission for Bill. But during the title search, it was discovered that there was a restriction on what could be built on the land, and the Meredith Corporation, which had owned the land Pomerantz had bought, held the right to approve what was built there.[6]

Ruan was going to back out of the deal if the restriction remained, and Bill sent Bill II to Pomerantz's attorney to get it lifted. Pomerantz, however, took the position that when he bought the land, he bought the right to approve what was built across the street. Seething, Bill saw Pomerantz's stand as a personal attack, and he filed a lawsuit to get the restriction removed. The two sides finally settled out of court, the restriction was lifted, and the Ruan deal closed in 1979, but the divide between Bill and Pomerantz deepened.

The two remained at odds for more than twenty years until roughly 2000, when both were evidently ready to put their resentments aside. It is not clear who made the first overture, but the two started going to lunch again. They did not discuss business much and no longer did deals together, but they were friends again and remained so until Pomerantz died in 2008.[7]

"REAL ESTATE IS RISKY: DO WHAT YOU CAN TO DECREASE RISKS"

Chapter Eight

Many people gamble in the real estate business and assume too much risk. Never take a risk that you are not willing to lose, and lessen risk whenever possible. Over his career, Bill did so by developing partnerships and avoiding too much debt.

Bill's efforts to decrease risk and assert control were responses to his childhood and the vagaries of farming, where outside factors such as weather, interest rates, and commodity prices often determined success or failure. Even though he had been drawn into an inherently unpredictable business, Bill always sought to reduce the capricious nature of real estate and the land development business.

By the late 1950s, Bill had discovered that partnering with others allowed him to become involved in even more deals, further lessening his risks by spreading his money across a variety of different investments. Today, roughly half his property is owned with one or two others. As noted earlier, Bill's first important partners were John Grubb and Hy-Vee Food Stores. Hy-Vee remains a significant partner today, while the others include the Farm Bureau, the National Chiropractic Malpractice Insurance Company, Unity Point Health, and good friend and former cable executive Jim Cownie. Also crucial to his success was his partnership in the 1980s with Roger Brooks and Central Life Assurance.[1]

In selecting partners, Bill was careful to work solely with people who possessed staying power and a lot of capital. "What you don't want," he explains, "is a partner who stays in when times are good but will pull out when things turn sour."[2]

Bill also understood that debt could be dangerous, and as a rule he paid cash for non-income-producing properties and in general kept leverage to a minimum. Liquidity was important in the business, especially in land development projects, where it could take a long time to complete the infrastructure, and in the meantime the market could change for the worse. "We take risks," Bill notes, "but if the projects don't go as planned, we're okay. I don't ever do a deal where if I made a mistake, I'd have to start over. I never wanted to start over."[3]

"BE PREPARED FOR BAD TIMES"

Chapter Nine

Good times do not last forever. Set aside enough cash in reserves to cover operating expenses to get you through prolonged recessions.

Bill and Iowa Realty had great success making money. Still, like many self-made businesspeople, Bill was often troubled by the fear of losing it all, but he knew little about preserving wealth or maintaining a firm during deep business slumps. Over the years, he had borrowed much of his money from Des Moines Savings and Loan, and its president, Dick Bryan, knew Bill's concerns and his financial situation. During a summer 1972 meeting, Bryan told him he was not sure that Bill or the firm could withstand a steep economic decline. He arranged for Bill to meet with James Downs Jr., a Chicago-based economist and renowned real estate consultant, to develop a plan for dealing with recessions.[1]

Bill and his accountant, Jack Wahlig, visited with Downs that fall, and he reiterated what Bryan had said. The real estate business was cyclical, Downs emphasized, and Bill and Iowa Realty were woefully unprepared for prolonged downturns in the market. To remedy the situation, Downs recommended that Iowa Realty maintain cash reserves large enough to cover all overhead expenses and loan payments for a two-year period. The statement jolted Bill and Wahlig. "This was a shock. We didn't keep a hell of a lot of cash in the bank because it was all invested in real estate," Bill recalled. Nonetheless, he took the counsel seriously and assiduously began setting aside money for the reserve fund.[2]

The advice proved crucial. By the end of the decade, an economic slowdown engulfed the nation, and the Des Moines housing market was hit hard. Iowa Realty saw its sales volume fall by nearly 20 percent from 1979 to 1980. Tough times continued, and real estate firms in the city declined by more than 30 percent from 1983 to 1985. Iowa Realty survived by cutting staff, shelving development projects, and relying on the cushion of the reserve fund Bill had created a decade earlier.[3]

Bill had always been interested in controlling situations, and maintaining a reserve fund fit well within his approach to business. It was a way for him to insulate himself against the vicissitudes of the real estate market.

"COURT THE MEDIA"

Chapter Ten

Newspapers and other media are always looking for a story. Be accessible, always treat newspeople with respect, and they will give you the benefit of the doubt.

Over the years, Bill was often one of the first people journalists turned to for stories on the local real estate industry, land development projects, or the continuing renewal of Des Moines's downtown core. His status as a leading business figure and his longtime involvement in the community were reasons enough for the media to seek him out, but it was more than that. Rather than shy away from reporters, Bill always returned their phone calls, and he became one of the few who regularly gave newspeople his cell phone number. But whenever possible, he visited with them in person. He was always up to date on the topics at hand and frequently provided good quotes, often saying something pithy in a common, even folksy manner.

What Bill refused to do was say anything negative about others in the press, even when pushed to do so. Once, for instance, he was asked about another wealthy civic leader, who, the reporter noted, seemed incredibly stingy when it came to charitable giving. While he agreed with the journalist's assessment, Bill offered a positive spin: "He doesn't give money now, but just wait until the right project comes along, and he will give big."[1]

Besides becoming a media favorite of sorts within greater Des Moines, Bill personally enjoyed favorable coverage. While the press admonished Iowa Realty or Knapp Properties from time to time, it almost never went after Bill personally. The one big exception to this involved the investigative pieces that *Des Moines Register* reporters ran about a transaction Bill and Denny Elwell had collaborated on in Ankeny.[2]

In 1999, Bill and Elwell bought eighty-four acres of land at roughly $15,000 per acre from the bankrupt Ankeny–Des Moines Aviation Exposition, which had held annual air shows there with radio-controlled model aircraft reenacting famous military battles. Five years later, in 2004, the partners sold seven acres of the land for $130,000 per acre to the Iowa Department of Transportation for a new driver's license facility.[3]

But shortly thereafter, a controversy erupted when Bert Dalmer and Tim Higgins, two *Des Moines Register* reporters, wrote an in-depth series of articles raising questions about the two transactions. They suggested that the 1999 transaction was an insider deal because Bill's brother, Paul, had been president of Aviation Expo, and Bill had had access to information about the land sale not privy to others. The reporters also noted that Gerry Neugent, then the president of Knapp Properties, had also served as the attorney for the expo. Moreover, Jeff Segin, a Knapp Properties broker, had marketed the land but acted on behalf of buyers Bill and Elwell as well. Finally, Dalmer and Higgins said that the sale had not been publicly announced, nor had the land ever been appraised, which raised questions about whether fair market value had been paid for it.[4]

The journalists also took issue with the relationship between Mark Wandro, the assistant Polk County engineer and then head of the Iowa Department of Transportation, and Bill and Elwell. Wandro was involved in laying out a new Interstate 35 interchange to be constructed near the Aviation Expo land shortly before Bill and Elwell purchased it. Then, as the director of the DOT, he rejected fifteen proposals for a new driver's license station before buying the seven acres at the new interstate interchange in Ankeny from Bill and Elwell.[5]

Bill was furious about the articles, which he felt were unjustified attacks, and in an unusual move he wrote a guest editorial defending himself and his firm. He was even willing to let the DOT out of the deal. Meanwhile Tom Miller, the Iowa attorney general, opened an investigation into the initial sale between the expo and Bill and Elwell, and David Vaudt, the state auditor, was considering whether an additional investigation was needed.[6]

By the spring of 2006, the attorney general's office had finished its inquiry and concluded that no state laws had been broken. But Vaudt had decided that the issue required further review, and his follow-up investigation lasted until the next summer, when it also found that the transaction did not violate any ethical or legal standards. Bill, of course, was pleased with the vindication, but he was irked that the *Register* devoted only four short paragraphs to the story.[7]

He kept these feelings to himself and remained available to the press. Soon the long-standing relationship he had built with the media in general and the *Register* in particular returned to normal. In January 2008, the paper ran a positive full-page story by business columnist Dave Elbert about Bill, his impact on the community, and his sale of the Knapp Properties management company to Bill II and Gerry Neugent.[8]

PART TWO
Where Credit Is Due

Bill Knapp's great success was nothing short of amazing. His drive and determination combined with his uncommon intelligence and entrepreneurial sense propelled the once poor farm boy rapidly up the socioeconomic ladder. But this "scrappy self-made real estate tycoon," in the words of his good friend David Kruidenier, the former publisher of the *Des Moines Register* and *Tribune*, recognized that he had more than his share of help throughout his career. Over the years many good people worked with Bill, while others gave him worthwhile advice or collaborated with him on profitable deals. A much smaller number proved essential, assisting him or shaping his thinking at crucial points in his life. These key friends, family members, colleagues, and one company helped Bill develop into the leading business and philanthropic figure he is today.[1]

IRENE KNAPP

Chapter Eleven

Irene Knapp, 2012. Courtesy of Irene Knapp.

Bill's initial partnership—the one that got him started—was his relationship with his first wife, Irene Knapp. The two met at Allerton High School in 1942, when Bill was a junior and Irene Hill was a sophomore. They became serious as Bill's graduation neared, but World War II interrupted their future together. He joined the U.S. Navy in July 1944 and served in the Pacific theater, seeing action at the Battle of Okinawa, where he piloted a landing craft and ferried Marines to and from the fight.[1]

The couple stayed in touch during the war, and when Bill was discharged two years later, he and Irene picked up where they had left off. They married in November 1946 and settled in Allerton, where Bill had a job at the milk plant, and Irene worked for the Wayne County Treasurer.[2]

Bill's position at the Allerton Co-op Dairy was the first of several menial, short-term positions he held to avoid returning to the farm, but his frequent moving from job to job created uncertainty and weighed on Irene. She encouraged him to take advantage of the GI Bill and go to vocational school, which she believed would help him find a satisfying career. Bill took her advice and got a bookkeeping job in 1949 after attending the American Institute of Business in Des Moines. Although happenstance intervened and Bill found his calling in real estate, Irene's guidance had broken her husband's cycle of hopping from one unsatisfying, unskilled job to another.[3]

Once in real estate, Bill relied even more heavily on Irene. As she recalled, "Bill was a lot like his father, and he wanted to be out working all the time." Such effort and initiative were good for his business, but they meant that he was not involved with household chores and did not spend much time with the couple's first child, Virginia Irene, who was born in September 1950. These duties fell to Irene, who happily took up the decade's stereotypical role of full-time homemaker once Ginny was born.[4]

But she did much more than that. The couple rarely socialized because of Bill's single-minded devotion to business, and when they did get together with friends, these were largely Bill's colleagues in the real estate world. Many of these gatherings were spontaneous—Bill would often call Irene in the late afternoon and explain that he was bringing several businesspeople over for dinner. After scrambling several times to throw together such meals, Irene began keeping extra food at the house for Bill's frequent requests for last-minute dinner parties.[5]

As Iowa Realty grew, Irene's role expanded beyond her domestic duties. When the company began selling homeowner's insurance in the early 1950s, Bill looked to Irene, who had held several bookkeeping positions and had an affinity for numbers, to direct the business. She ran the operation out of the family's basement, and Bill hired Beatrice Turner to clean their home once a week. It soon became clear that Irene needed to devote more time to the growing business, and Turner began working full-time for the Knapps, cleaning and helping care for young Ginny.[6]

Bea Turner stayed on at the Knapps, and before long Irene took on an even more important position at the company. In 1957, there was a small fire at the Iowa Realty office; fortunately, damage was limited solely to the desk and work space of bookkeeper Jo Ann Burman, and business was uninterrupted. However, an investigation indicated that Burman had been embezzling and had started the blaze to destroy evidence of her wrongdoing. When Bill confronted her, she confessed to both crimes. He fired her. But this left him wanting someone he could trust to oversee the company's books, and he looked to Irene. She stepped into the job, and her growing insurance business was moved into the office where Joe Clay, Iowa Realty's closing manager, headed it.[7]

Here again, Irene helped Bill when he needed it, capably handling the bookkeeping duties for almost two years before becoming pregnant. The couple's son, Roger Bill, was born in September 1959. After this, Irene did not work at Iowa Realty again, but she continued to personify the woman behind the man.[8]

Irene was content being a full-time wife and mother, managing their home, raising their children, and supporting Bill in his career ambitions. Even though she was shy and generally quiet, Irene spent years dutifully accompanying Bill to a growing number of business and social events, where he schmoozed with colleagues, possible customers, and potential partners. But she tired of these gatherings, and as she became busier with Roger and his growing interest in tennis, she stopped attending many such events, and Bill went on his own.[9]

By this time, Ginny was married and out of the house, and Roger's success in tennis took up more and more of Irene's time. In 1972, the youngster won the regional twelve-and-under tournament, and over the next few years Irene took him to matches throughout the Midwest. She even developed a sophisticated scoring system that tracked his serves, shots, and general play in each tournament. Roger became the first freshman to win the state high school tennis tournament, and he defended his title the next year.[10]

It was now apparent that Roger wanted to play tennis professionally. Arden Stokstad, his tennis instructor, told Bill and Irene that their son had the talent and the temperament to pursue his dream but needed a top coach and access to year-round outdoor tennis. The couple agreed, and ultimately Roger and Irene moved to La Jolla, a wealthy coastal village north of San Diego, where he enrolled as a junior in high school. Several times a week, Irene drove him twenty miles north to the La Costa Resort in Carlsbad, where he took private lessons with Pancho Segura, a top professional tennis player in the 1940s and 1950s and then a leading teaching professional and coach to the likes of Jimmy Connors and Stan Smith.[11]

Irene and Bea Turner, who had known Roger since he was born, arranged a system so that one of them would always be with the high schooler in La Jolla. Irene lived there for six to eight weeks at a time before returning to Des Moines, when she was replaced in southern California by Turner. Bill generally flew out a couple of times a month, and daughter Ginny, who had given birth to the Knapps' first grandchild in 1974, often visited with her young daughter, Kendy.[12]

Not surprisingly, the arrangement strained the relationship between Bill and Irene, and it was during these couple of years in La Jolla that Ginny and Roger, then Turner and Irene, surmised that Bill and Connie Wimer, a longtime friend and the wife of Bill's attorney Bill Wimer, were having an affair. Their suspicions proved correct, but when Irene confronted Bill, he denied it. After asking about it several more times and receiving the same answer, Irene dropped the subject, hoping the relationship would soon end. She remained patient with Bill, but the affair continued. Bill wanted to keep his family intact, but he also wanted to continue seeing Connie. The situation dragged on for another decade until the Knapps' marriage finally ended in 1986, when Bill moved out. Their divorce became final the following year.[13]

Irene received a generous settlement, which provided her with an affluent lifestyle, but she was understandably angry. "You can't help but be bitter when you went through those years and struggled to get ahead.

You didn't have anything at all, and you raised the kids. Then about the time when you can have something, they go off with someone else." Bill felt guilty about breaking up his marriage and disrupting his family, but he needed to move on. Yet he never lost sight of all Irene had done for him during the lean years while he was building Iowa Realty. She had been supportive and understanding of Bill's all-consuming commitment to the business, managed their home, and raised their children, and she had twice stepped in to handle jobs at the firm.[14]

KENNY GRANDQUIST

Chapter Twelve

Kenny Grandquist, 1998. Courtesy of Linda Grandquist.

In Kenny Grandquist, Bill found just the right person to help him build Iowa Realty into the state's leading real estate firm. The two met in 1949, when Bill called Grandquist's gas station at the corner of Thirtieth Street and Hickman Road about getting his stalled car started. Grandquist went out and got the car going, then asked if Bill ever needed gas. From then on, Bill bought all his gas at Grandquist's Phillips 66 service station. As the two became friendly, he saw Grandquist's aptitude for sales and offered him a job at Iowa Realty. Bill finally persuaded his friend to make the move, and Grandquist joined the company in the summer of 1953.[1]

Grandquist did not disappoint. He was immediately "selling like hell" and quickly became Iowa Realty's leading salesman. But more importantly, the ebullient and fun-loving Grandquist was well liked and respected at the firm and soon became its informal sales manager. His natural ability for managing people was also important because this was not Bill's strong suit. The position became formalized in 1956, and a clear division of labor between the two soon developed: Grandquist oversaw the sales side of the company, while Bill searched for new opportunities.[2]

One of the first changes Grandquist initiated as sales manager was the introduction of weekly sales meetings. Such meetings became imperative as the company grew and the casual conversations or informal meetings that once disseminated information were no longer adequate. Grandquist was at his best on this stage, serving as teacher, promoter, and communicator. Here he encouraged his sales staff, offered tips on moving homes, provided updates on company policies, and fielded questions and complaints.[3]

Because Bill understood Grandquist's significance to the operation, he started giving him Iowa Realty stock in the late 1950s as an incentive to stay with the company and work to expand it. But he also genuinely liked Grandquist, and the two became close friends. A few months before Grandquist began at Iowa Realty, in the spring of 1953, Bill and Irene moved to a house on Clinton Street in Des Moines's Beaverdale neighborhood, which happened to be down the street from Kenny and Evelyn Grandquist's house. The families were soon seeing a lot of each other, and later that summer Iowa Realty moved into a new office building—constructed by Grandquist's builder father, Olaf—on Beaver Avenue, half a mile away from their homes.[4]

Being only a few blocks away from the office was especially handy because as Bill recalled, "business came first," and he and Grandquist were usually at the building seven days a week. Bill often went home for dinner, but he generally returned to the office, and he and Grandquist frequently worked there until 10 or 11 p.m.[5]

Bill and Irene briefly left the neighborhood in 1957, moving to a larger home in Windsor Heights, a suburb several miles southwest of Beaverdale. Although it was still just a short drive from the new house to Iowa Realty's office, its location was not nearly as convenient, and Bill started skipping family dinners and staying at the office. This bothered Irene, who enjoyed fixing a big evening meal and having Bill at home. So after only a few months, the Knapps decided to return to the old neighborhood and build a new home down the street from the former one.[6]

In the meantime, the Grandquists were also thinking about a larger home. Grandquist and Bill began talking and decided to build new homes adjacent to each other on Clinton Street. They chose identical floor plans, and Grandquist's father built both split-levels. Seven years later, they repeated the process, building much bigger homes next door to each other on Beaver Avenue between Aurora and Madison Avenues. The homes were in the first plat carved out of the former Meredith estate, which Bill and John Grubb had recently purchased.[7]

The connection between the two had grown even closer when they founded United Investments, a partnership distinct from Iowa Realty designed to build or buy and hold investment properties. These included several apartment buildings, beginning with their 1962 construction of such a structure on the corner of Sixty-Third Street and Hickman Road, a few miles to the northwest of downtown Des Moines.[8]

All was going well for the close friends. They had the same ideas about making money and building Iowa Realty, and these shared dreams and their compatibility made them nearly inseparable. "If you saw Bill," real estate agent Roger Cleven observed, "you knew Kenny wasn't far behind."[9]

Iowa Realty boomed under Grandquist's leadership. Residential sales more than tripled, moving from $7.85 million in 1957 to $26 million in 1970, while the number of agents at the firm increased from twenty-one to fifty-two over the same period.[10]

Yet by the early 1970s Bill's brother, Paul Knapp, then Iowa Realty's assistant manager, was becoming exasperated with Grandquist, who he thought was growing complacent about the company's operations. Others sensed this as well. Daryl Neumann, who had joined Iowa Realty as its controller in early 1972, noted, for instance, "Ken was not as energetic and ambitious as he was in the earlier days. I think this was slowing down the growth of the company."[11]

Grandquist and Paul had a serious disagreement about the size of the firm. Paul proposed doubling the sales force to counter the rapid growth of local rival Stanbrough Realty, but Grandquist thought the firm should stick with the current number of skilled agents instead of adding many more, which would certainly include a number of mediocre ones. Paul was also disgruntled because as long as Grandquist was vice president and general manager, he did not have a clear path to advance in the company.[12]

At the end of 1972, Paul took these frustrations to Bill and threatened to quit. After a difficult conversation, Bill ultimately agreed with his brother, but he did not want to lose Grandquist or jeopardize their friendship. He appointed Grandquist president of the company, overseeing its commercial operations; he took the title of chairman; and he promoted Paul to vice president and general sales manager heading up residential real estate.[13]

Bill hoped that the reorganization would work and that Grandquist would stay with Iowa Realty. He initially did, but it was obvious that their relationship had changed. The two avoided each other whenever possible, and Grandquist soon left the company's main Beaverdale office for its commercial real estate office on Ingersoll Avenue. Then, symbolic of the growing chasm between them, Grandquist ended the awkward situation of being next-door neighbors with the Knapps by moving to a new home. But he remained angry about how he had been treated. Although his title suggested that he had been promoted, many in the industry considered it a demotion, and Grandquist believed it to be a dead-end job. He left Iowa Realty in early 1977 and created a competitor, Universal Realty. Hostility between the two mounted, but they were finally able to make amends in the mid-1980s. They eventually returned to being next-door neighbors again, but by then Grandquist had divorced Evelyn and married businesswoman and real estate agent Linda Holmes.[14]

Meanwhile, Grandquist had become involved in Des Moines's minor-league baseball team, and by the late 1990s he was the majority owner of the Iowa Cubs, the triple-A affiliate of the Chicago Cubs. Tragically, he suffered a stroke while watching their home opener at Sec Taylor Stadium (now Principal Park) in April 1999. He was rushed to Iowa Methodist Medical Center (now part of Unity Point Health), but he never regained consciousness. Bill and Susan hurried to the hospital when they heard the news, and they returned to sit with Grandquist and Linda every day for the next week until he passed away.[15]

Grandquist's death was difficult for Bill. He had faced the death of family members and other friends before, but this loss was different. Simply put, Grandquist had been indispensable to the maturation of Iowa Realty, and for years he had been Bill's closest friend. Fortunately, three days before the stroke, Bill and Paul had lunch with Grandquist and his brother, John, at the Cub Club restaurant at the ballpark. There Bill and Grandquist reminisced, sharing many fond memories of their intimately intertwined careers. "We didn't realize it at the time," Bill recalled, "but our lunch was like a final farewell."[16]

PAUL KNAPP

Chapter Thirteen

Bill and Paul Knapp, 1995. Courtesy of Bill Knapp.

If Kenny Grandquist was the sparkplug that helped ignite the early growth and development of Iowa Realty's residential sales, Paul Knapp was the turbocharger that fueled its rapid expansion, taking the company's brokerage business to an entirely new level. Yet Paul's significance went well beyond that. Jim Hubbell III, then president of local competitor Hubbell Realty, explained, "Bill's style requires somebody that runs the company on a day-to-day basis. He brings in an enormous amount of business, and he needs someone to execute that and take care of details. He's very fortunate to have a brother, someone he knows extremely well and has faith in, and Paul's a tremendous asset to the company." Bill said it more simply, "We couldn't have done half of the things we've done if it hadn't been for Paul."[1]

Separated by only seventeen months, the Knapp brothers had been especially close since childhood, but they were different from the very beginning. Bill was short and tough, brash and outgoing, while Paul would grow bigger and taller but was more cautious and reticent than his older brother. Nonetheless, whether at work or play, the two were nearly inseparable, with Bill leading and Paul following. This pattern would continue for most of their lives. Once back in Des Moines after a two-year stint in the Navy, Paul learned that Bill planned to attend the American Institute of Business, and he enrolled in the vocational school as well.[2]

In 1950, shortly after Bill went into real estate, Paul got his real estate license, and he sold homes part-time until he found a full-time job in sales at Massey Harris (this would become Massey Ferguson in 1958), a farm implement maker. His career was interrupted in 1951, when the Navy called him up during the Korean War. He returned in 1953, went back to Massey Harris, and was soon promoted to zone sales manager. But when he was transferred to the Oskaloosa office, he began looking for another job that would bring him back to Des Moines. Ironically, it was Kenny Grandquist who suggested that Iowa Realty hire him. Bill agreed; he believed that he and his brother could work well together.[3]

Paul joined Iowa Realty in 1956, and with his sales experience and connections, he had an immediate impact. He initially sold many expensive homes to managers he knew at Massey Ferguson and went on to become one of the firm's leading agents. As he had been since childhood, Paul remained Bill's closest confidant, and somehow the brothers' tight bond did not create friction with Grandquist. In fact, Paul and Grandquist became good friends inside and outside the office as well. All three evidently understood where they fit in the company hierarchy and were satisfied with their positions. As Grandquist noted, "I never had any trouble with Paul trying to edge in on me."[4]

Thus, a trio of friendships developed. Bill, Paul, and Grandquist participated in a bowling league in the late 1950s and were part of a group that played tennis together. They also all joined Des Moines's Scottish Rite Masons. Meanwhile, Paul and Grandquist often played golf together. These outings irritated Bill, who detested golf for years and saw it as a waste of time. Instead, he thought, the two should be rubbing shoulders with potential customers or clients.[5]

The three colleagues grew that much closer when Paul moved his family to a larger home on Beaver Avenue in 1966, several doors down the block from Grandquist and Bill. And when all three were in the office, they regularly lunched together at the Mandarin restaurant across the street.[6]

This all changed in late 1972, when Bill agreed with Paul's ideas to expand Iowa Realty and promoted him to head the residential brokerage business. Unlike Grandquist, who had managed through charm, charisma, or intimidation if needed, Paul was quiet, reserved, and thoughtful, relying on his vast knowledge of the industry to direct the operation. He focused on the organizational structure, controller Daryl Neumann noted, and "was much more likely to work closely with agents on the nitty-gritty details."[7]

When Paul took control, Iowa Realty had sixty-five agents spread across five branch offices in greater Des Moines. Convinced that a larger sales force and more branches would mean greater sales, he began a rapid expansion. By the end of 1980, the firm boasted thirty-three branches, including offices in the surrounding towns of Guthrie Center, Ames, Boone, Perry, and Nevada, and 268 residential agents, a fourfold increase in just eight years. Just as he expected, revenues soared, increasing to $121 million, up nearly five times since 1970.[8]

Paul had even bigger plans. He wanted to extend the company's reach across the entire state and convinced Bill that franchising was the way to do it. The first franchise was established in Marshalltown, fifty miles northeast of Des Moines, in the spring of 1980, and from there blue and white Iowa Realty signs began spreading outward from the capital city across the state. Bill was delighted; such growth provided him with more money for real estate deals.[9]

Paul oversaw residential sales as general sales manager until 1980, when Clair Niday, a brother-in-law of Bill's, took over the day-to-day operations. Paul soon moved up to president and became more involved in developing long-term strategy for the firm.[10]

However, he played a much bigger role than merely overseeing the residential sales business. He managed the company's many large developments and bought properties. Even more importantly, Bill had complete confidence in him and consulted him daily about potential new projects and possible deals. Paul once explained how the two were able to work so well together: "I understand who the boss is, and I have no problems with that whatsoever. I think his judgment is good, and he respects me and lets me do my job." Bill, in turn, knew how lucky he was to have Paul with him at Iowa Realty. At Christmas 1986, he gave his brother a plaque that read, "Paul: My little big brother—who has stood beside me and behind me—for all these many years, I humbly thank you."[11]

Bill later expounded: "Paul's been a reliable partner, one I could trust, and we've always had a great working relationship. I never had to worry about turning my back, and I always knew if there was a problem, he'd let me know about it. Besides being brothers, we've been good friends. He's just always been there. Steady. Strong. We respect each other and we try to do each other right."[12]

Paul continued moving up in Iowa Realty until he was named chairman in 1995, when Bill became chairman emeritus. Two years later, in 1997, Paul retired. In 2008, roughly a decade later, after dealing with declining health for several years, Paul died. Dwayne McAninch, an earthmoving contractor and longtime friend of the two Knapps, commented on their special relationship, "I don't know two brothers who appreciated each other more than those two."[13]

JOHN R. GRUBB

Chapter Fourteen

John R. Grubb, circa 1993. Courtesy of John W. Grubb.

Des Moines builder John R. Grubb may have been the first friend of Bill's to become a customer and partner. He was certainly the most important such figure early in Bill's career. Like many homebuilders at the time, Grubb had started small. Shortly after returning from service in World War II, he borrowed money, built two homes, sold them, and with the profits bought another lot and began to repeat the process. Early success and the great postwar demand for homes meant that Grubb's operation soon grew, and he started constructing more and more homes. Grubb relied on Byron Hollis to sell some of his properties, and it was here at the Hollis realty firm that Grubb first met Bill.[1]

The two came from similar backgrounds. Both had grown up poor, both had fought in World War II, and both had tried several jobs before serendipitously finding their callings. They became immediate friends and were soon socializing together with their wives. Predictably, business quickly entered the mix as well.[2]

In 1958, Grubb was developing his first subdivision, Zelda Acres, named in honor of his wife, on land just south of Resthaven Cemetery in West Des Moines. Iowa Realty had enjoyed success selling many of Grubb's homes, so the builder looked to his friend and the firm to handle the sale of the development's lots and homes. Bill ran an eye-catching half-page ad in the *Des Moines Register* offering Grubb's sixty-eight three-bedroom brick homes, ranging in price from $16,650 to $21,900: "The Most Revolutionary Home Buy Ever in the History of Des Moines and It's Here for You Now in ZELDA ACRES. VETERANS! No Down Payment." They held three open houses, with balloons festively decorating the completed show homes. Iowa Realty agents were on hand and sold nineteen homes that first weekend. A month later, all the completed homes as well as those under construction had been sold, while most of those yet to be built had been presold.[3]

The success at Zelda Acres enhanced the reputations of both Grubb and Bill and led the friends into more partnerships. In 1959, Grubb announced Sheridan Park, a much larger subdivision with 550 modest homes northeast of downtown Des Moines, and he again looked to Bill to market the development. Just like Zelda Acres, the deal was highly profitable for both Grubb and Iowa Realty.[4]

That same year, Bill bought Stuart Hills, a thirty-acre parcel just to the west of the new Merle Hay Plaza scheduled to open that August. Shortly after the purchase, he and Grubb formed Allied Development, a fifty-fifty partnership to hold land, and transferred Stuart Hills to the new entity. Stuart Hills was a prime piece of real estate, and Bill sold all the lots before the subdivision's streets were built. Then the two founded Alcon Construction. It erected several buildings, including, for example, a Kentucky Fried Chicken franchise and an office building along Douglas Avenue between Sixty-Third and Sixty-Fourth Streets as well as apartments that Bill and Grandquist had initially owned.[5]

Meanwhile, Bill had gotten the best of Grubb in a farcical deal that the two laughed about for years. In 1956, Bill's financial success led him to upgrade his car from an Oldsmobile to a Cadillac, the ultimate status symbol of the decade. It was a showy bright purple convertible. His friends called it the purple ghost, and soon the flamboyant color was too much for Bill. He ordered a new one in a subdued shade in 1958, but a strike at General Motors slowed production and delayed the auto's delivery date. Grubb had already received his new Cadillac and drove it over to Iowa Realty to show it off. He took Bill for a drive in the new car, and Bill asked how much Grubb would charge him to trade cars now and take Bill's new Cadillac when it arrived. Grubb thought he was being facetious and chose the ridiculously high figure of $2,500. Bill agreed, and when they stopped at a light, he reached over, took the keys from the ignition, and told Grubb to get out of his car. Grubb chuckled, but Bill was serious and said they had made a deal. Grubb finally got out of the car, walked back to the Iowa Realty office, and took the purple ghost home. He drove it for several months until his new Cadillac arrived.[6]

Beyond the deals, the two saw each other frequently. Much of their time together was spent at the Zodiac Club, a favorite spot for those involved in real estate, located in the basement of the Commodore Hotel at Grand Avenue and Thirty-Fifth Street. Likewise, as Scottish Rite Masons and Za-Ga-Zig Shriners, they regularly socialized at fraternal functions. Later, starting in the late 1970s, both Grubb and Bill were part of a prayer group made up of some of the city's most prominent business leaders. It met Thursday mornings for breakfast and included banker David Miller, Dwight Swanson, president of Iowa Power and Light Company, Fred Weitz, head of the Weitz Company, attorney Tom Flynn, and broadcast executive Tom Stoner. Former governor Harold Hughes occasionally attended as well.[7]

But business remained a big part of their relationship, and the two continued doing real estate ventures together. Most notable were their purchase and then development of the Meredith estate, but there were many others, including the 1984 acquisition of West Des Moines State Bank (now West Bank), where Bill and David Miller recruited Grubb to be part of the consortium purchasing the institution. They also worked together on a big philanthropic project, joining several other business leaders in developing Des Moines's Gray's Lake Park, southwest of downtown, which opened in 2001.[8]

Several years before Grubb died in 2003, Bill described his special relationship with the builder: "John's been a great friend for over forty years, and Iowa Realty's longest, most consistent customer. We've been competitors and partners and have made every kind of deal imaginable. I give him a lot of credit for our success."[9]

HY-VEE FOOD STORES

Chapter Fifteen

Hy-Vee Food Stores, one of Bill's oldest partners. The image is of the company's old-time logo inside its downtown Des Moines store. Courtesy of Hy-Vee, Inc.

Hy-Vee is the lone company on this list because, as Bill explained in 2017, "We have a lot of partners, but Hy-Vee is the best partner we have in everything we do," and it is with Hy-Vee that Bill has had his longest continuous business relationship.[1]

Bill worked briefly with Hy-Vee (then called the Supply Store) in the late 1940s, when he and Irene ran their Allerton café, and they bought all their food from the grocer. As he recalls, David Vredenburg (one of the founders) personally delivered meat and produce to the Knapps' restaurant.[2]

A little over a decade later Hy-Vee, then based in the southern Iowa town of Chariton, fifty miles south of Des Moines, was looking to put its grocery stores in the capital city. In 1959, the company opened a store in the northern suburb of Johnston, and the following year company CEO Dwight Vredenburg sent Harold Trumbull, its vice president overseeing real estate, to check out potential sites for markets in Des Moines. During his search he met Bill, and the two began discussing properties in the area. Soon Bill had negotiated two deals with Trumbull and Hy-Vee. Allied Development, Bill's partnership with Grubb, would build the grocery stores to Hy-Vee's specifications on property it owned in Urbandale, at 6501 Douglas Avenue, and in northeast Des Moines, on 2537 East Euclid Street. Alcon Construction, another Knapp-Grubb joint venture, erected the buildings, and when completed in 1961 they were leased to Hy-Vee.[3]

The lease arrangement proved rewarding and fit well within Bill's willingness to wait for profits, but it did not coincide with Grubb's business style, and in 1964 Bill bought out his partner's share of Allied Development as well as his portion of Alcon Construction. But Bill's relationship with Hy-Vee only grew.[4]

In the late 1970s, Hy-Vee was outgrowing its store on Twenty-Second Street in West Des Moines and was looking for a larger facility. The company again turned to Bill, who soon found the ideal spot for another store on Iowa Realty land. He constructed a building to Hy-Vee's specifications on Thirty-Fifth Street (now Valley West Drive) across from the newly opened Valley West Mall and leased it to the grocer in 1979. That deal led to two others. Bill negotiated a bargain with Service Merchandise (now a Goodwill store) to build and then lease the retailer a structure directly south of the new Hy-Vee, and he sold the rest of the parcel north of Hy-Vee to Target, which built a large store there.[5]

At about the same time, Bill bought three Hy-Vee store buildings in eastern Iowa—two in Davenport and one in Mt. Pleasant—which he then leased to the grocer. The relationship continued to pay big dividends. In 1988, Hy-Vee bought twenty-one acres in what was then called Country Club business park in West Des Moines for its new corporate headquarters, and it also purchased Iowa Realty land at the corner of University Avenue and Seventy-Fourth Street (now Jordan Creek Parkway) for a new grocery store. A little over a decade later, Bill built a Drug Town (a Hy-Vee subsidiary; the outlets were later renamed Hy-Vee Drugstores) on his land at Sixtieth Street and Ashworth Road in West Des Moines and leased it to the company.[6]

"We've had a very profitable relationship with Hy-Vee over the decades. They run a first-class operation, and whether it was Dwight Vredenburg or the later CEOs such as Ron Pearson, Ric Jurgens, or now Randy Edeker, they've been great to work with." But possibly Bill's favorite Hy-Vee deal started with a meeting he had in 2013. Over lunch, Edeker told him that he wanted to build a grocery store in downtown Des Moines, and he wanted Knapp Properties to join them in the venture. Bill was immediately interested and agreed to work with his old partner.[7]

Bill had played a prominent role in downtown Des Moines's revitalization, which began in earnest in the 1970s and 1980s. This renaissance included gleaming new office towers, the Civic Center, Nollen Plaza (now Cowles Commons), the high-rise Marriott Hotel, and Bill's refurbished Hotel Savery, all connected by the growing skywalk system. But he understood that without housing downtown, "you've got a ghost town after 5 o'clock." He therefore became one of the biggest advocates of adding housing to the area, and over the period he was the key figure in bringing two apartment complexes and the Plaza condominiums to the city center.[8]

Bill realized that the missing element was a grocery store, but there were still not enough people living downtown to lure anyone to build such a market. He explained, "It's something we've wanted for years, but the timing never gets right until you have enough people." More and more housing went up in the downtown area after 2000, and by 2013 Randy Edeker believed that the critical mass was there to support a store. He also believed that Bill Knapp was exactly the right partner: "I think he's an incredible guy—self-made, hard-working; you know, visionary." Plus, Edeker knew Bill "had a passion to get a store downtown."[9]

After managers from Knapp Properties and Hy-Vee scouted several sites, Bill and Edeker settled on a two acre-parking lot at Fourth Street and Court Avenue, which the city had opened for development bids. Five were submitted. The Knapp Properties/Hy-Vee joint venture called for a first-floor grocery store, topped by apartments, and included an adjacent parking structure. Three other proposals were based around apartments, with one including space for an indoor farmers market, while the fifth proposed a luxury movie theater complex.[10]

The Des Moines City Council picked the Knapp/Hy-Vee project in early 2014. The partnership was given the land, and the building would be jointly owned. Hy-Vee would lease the ground floor from the partnership for the grocery, and Knapp Properties would manage the building. Construction crews began work in August 2015, and the highly anticipated downtown Hy-Vee opened in February 2017, while the eighty-two apartments above the supermarket were finished shortly thereafter. "The grocery store is a game changer for downtown," Bill observed. "It was a long time in coming. I'm glad we finally got it done, and I'm glad we got it done with Hy-Vee."[11]

BILL WIMER AND CONNIE WIMER

Chapter Sixteen

Bill Wimer, circa 1980.
Courtesy of Connie Wimer.

Connie Wimer, circa 1977.
Courtesy of Connie Wimer.

Both together and separately, Bill Wimer and Connie Wimer were significant in Bill's life for roughly thirty years. He noted, "The Wimers were important to me for a long time. They were my first friends who were socially polished, cultivated, and tied into Des Moines society. I'd been in the business world for ten or so years, but I was still just a raw, uneducated farm boy at heart. I was rough as hell. They expanded my horizons, especially to the world of ideas, style, and culture." Meanwhile, attorney Bill Wimer had become a key figure in Bill's business, serving as a confidant and doing most of Iowa Realty's legal work. Likewise, Connie grew close to Bill as well, and their relationship eventually evolved into a romantic affair that lasted nearly twenty years.[1]

Roy Riley, a relatively new agent at Iowa Realty, introduced Bill to Bill Wimer in 1956. Wimer was educated, well read, and urbane—everything Bill was not—but the two enjoyed an immediate rapport. Bill believed Wimer's expertise in real estate and zoning law as well as his connections with influential businesspeople would prove helpful. For Wimer, Bill was the rising star in local real estate who could provide him with a lot of business. The relationship proved to be mutually beneficial, and by the late 1950s Wimer was indeed opening doors for Bill and doing most of Iowa Realty's legal work.[2]

Wimer's extensive network kept him up to date on the disposition of various local properties, and as Bill had hoped, his lawyer passed this information along. It was Wimer, for instance, who told Bill that the Meredith estate was likely to be put up for sale. This led to his 1963 purchase of the property, his biggest deal to date. Later, Wimer advised Bill that the Savery was available for purchase, and Bill bought what became his beloved hotel.[3]

Besides keeping Bill well informed, Wimer followed up on all the deals he closed, tying up any loose ends, drafting contracts, and filing all the necessary paperwork. Sometimes Bill relied on Wimer to handle personal matters as well. In one instance, he sent Wimer to southern California to scout out housing and schools after the Knapps decided that son Roger needed to move to the West Coast to work under tennis pro Pancho Segura. As Bill II put it, "Bill didn't do anything without Bill Wimer."[4]

Although this was not clear at the time, Wimer trained Bill's next generation of colleagues as well. He convinced a young Bill II to go to law school, and then he hired him and fellow Drake law school student Gerry Neugent to clerk at his law firm, then called Stewart, Wimer and Bump. After finishing law school, Bill II remained with the firm a short time before moving to Iowa Realty as its in-house counsel. Neugent, on the other hand, stayed with Wimer for years; following his mentor's example, he became one of the city's leading real estate attorneys.[5]

While Bill Wimer became important to Bill's business career, he and his wife, Connie, played an essential role in his social maturation as well. Although Bill had risen rapidly in the world of real estate, he was often awkward and uncomfortable in social settings. His interactions with the Wimers began to change that. The Knapps and the Wimers became friendly in the 1960s, but Irene's involvement soon stopped because the couples' conversations often focused on business, which she found tiresome. Bill, however, reveled in the get-togethers and continued going out with the Wimers and attending their dinner parties. Time with the Wimers broadened Bill's then provincial outlook, improved his poor grammar, and introduced him to many of the city's prominent figures. He also began paying more attention to his attire, picking up style cues from Bill Wimer, generally regarded as one of the best-dressed men in Des Moines.[6]

Frequent interaction with the Wimers eventually led to Bill's long-standing affair with Connie, which began in the early 1970s, and both couples divorced the following decade. During Connie's divorce proceedings, Bill became angry with the way attorney Roger Hudson, one of Bill Wimer's law partners, was treating her, and he pulled all Iowa Realty's business from the firm. Shortly thereafter, partners Tom Flynn and Gerry Neugent left Wimer's firm to join what is now Belin McCormick, a larger Des Moines law firm. Because Neugent had been doing much of the Iowa Realty work while with Wimer, Bill moved the company's business to that firm.[7]

Bill and Connie's love affair eventually wound down, ending in 1992, but the two remained friends. The following year, sixty-three-year-old Bill Wimer died unexpectedly from complications of an aneurysm. In the meantime, Connie had continued her own climb in the Des Moines business world, which had begun in 1976 when she purchased Iowa Title Company. After building it into the city's largest abstracting firm, she sold it in 1985. At the same time, she had been branching out into publishing, buying the *Daily Record*, which ran legal notices. She soon rebranded it the *Business Record*, focusing on local business news. This became the basis for her successful and ever-expanding Business Publications Corporation. In 1998, she married Frank Fogarty, a retired Coca-Cola executive. Fogarty died in 2020.[8]

JACK WAHLIG

Chapter Seventeen

Jack Wahlig, 2013. Courtesy of Susan Knapp.

Bill always said that for a company to be successful, it "needed a good lawyer and a good accountant." By the late 1950s, he had found his attorney for Iowa Realty in Bill Wimer; several years later, he had his accountant in Jack Wahlig.[1]

Initially, Iowa Realty operated with only a bookkeeper, and Bill relied on the McGladrey firm (now RSM) to handle the company's accounting. Robert Timmons originally did the work, but in 1962 he took a job at Thermagas. McGladrey then transferred Jack Wahlig from Dubuque to replace Timmons and manage the Des Moines office. Wahlig also took over the Iowa Realty account. Bill had been perfectly happy with Timmons's work, but Wahlig soon filled much bigger shoes. Besides handling Iowa Realty's accounting needs as well as Bill's personal accounting work, he became a trusted financial adviser and business consultant for both Bill and his real estate business.[2]

Shortly after Wahlig arrived in Des Moines, banker David Miller, an old friend of his from eastern Iowa, recruited the accountant into the Breakfast Club, an organization that met weekly and offered prominent business leaders a place to socialize, build relationships, and negotiate deals. Wahlig was impressed with the group and thought Bill would benefit from it. He told Bill about it, and soon the real estate man was recruited into the club as well. Just as the accountant thought, Bill was soon building relationships and doing deals with fellow members.[3]

The Breakfast Club proved an important resource for Bill, but it was not nearly as consequential as his 1972 visit with real estate guru and economist James Downs Jr. Wahlig accompanied Bill to this Chicago meeting, where Downs told the two that Iowa Realty needed to maintain much more cash on hand to survive deep recessions. Both came out of the meeting stunned, but Bill was ready to follow this advice, and Wahlig developed the plan to do so. That meeting, in Wahlig's opinion, "was one of the keystones in Bill's career because he became very aware of not overextending." Bill saw the meeting as critical as well. "We weren't ready for steep declines in the market but got prepared after Downs talked to us. That may have been what saved us during the crunch in the early 1980s."[4]

According to Bill II, Wahlig "brought order to Iowa Realty" with his frequent "chalk talks," where he thought aloud at meetings while illustrating his ideas on a marker board. His thinking often led to long-term strategies as well as solutions to current problems. It was Wahlig, for example, who thought the bitter feud with Kenny Grandquist, which resulted in his lawsuit against Iowa Realty, was distracting and damaging to all. He pushed Bill "to give more than you must to settle," and such an agreement was finally reached between the two in 1979.[5]

In 1982, Wahlig became McGladrey's CEO and no longer did Iowa Realty's accounting work, but he remained one of Bill's go-to consultants. He was involved in three of Bill's biggest moves over the next decade: his sale of 80 percent of Iowa Realty in 1984, his sale of the remaining 20 percent of the firm in 1989, and the creation of Knapp Properties in 1992. Wahlig retired from McGladrey in 1995.

HAROLD HUGHES

Chapter Eighteen

Harold Hughes, 1967. Courtesy of the State Historical Society of Iowa, Des Moines.

Bill has known many politicians over the years, but the one who most impressed him and influenced him was Iowa governor and then U.S. senator Harold Hughes. The two met in 1962. Bill had heard a lot about the colorful gubernatorial candidate. Indeed, Hughes had a compelling story. A truck driver who battled and overcame alcoholism, he rose to head the state trucking association before his election to the Iowa Commerce Commission in 1958. From there, he launched his run for governor. Bill asked Lex Hawkins, the state Democratic chairman, to arrange a meeting. Hawkins agreed and brought Hughes by the Iowa Realty office. The tall, charismatic Hughes instantly won over Bill, who remembered immediately "liking him as a man." Shortly after the visit, Bill donated $1,000 to his campaign, which Hughes recalled as "a generous contribution at the time."[1]

The meeting marked the beginning of a close friendship between the businessman and the soon-to-be-elected Iowa governor. Hughes served in that capacity for three two-year terms before Robert Kennedy convinced him to run for the U.S. Senate, where he served until 1975. Bill played an important financial role in these campaigns, giving his own money and leading fundraising efforts. He also grew to be one of the few people with whom Hughes said he could "let his hair down."[2]

The two spent quite a bit of time together, sometimes hunting or fishing, two pastimes Hughes enjoyed but Bill only endured. "I remember sitting in duck blinds by the hours," Bill noted, "freezing to death, while he loved every minute of it." Likewise, when Hughes needed to get away to think or recharge, he could do so at the developer's Sugar Creek retreat west of Des Moines, which Bill made available to the governor.[3]

Through Hughes, Bill became acquainted with other prominent Democrats, including renowned lawyer and businessman Joe Rosenfield, businessman John Chrystal, congressman and then senator John Culver, and congressman Neal Smith. Likewise, his involvement with Hughes and his administrations embedded Bill in prominent Democratic circles, and he quickly developed into an important fundraiser and a generous supporter of the party. In fact, from the 1970s on, Bill "contributed more money to Iowa Democratic candidates and causes than anyone in the state." At the same time, he became an influential power broker in the state's Democratic Party. As the *Des Moines Register* reported in 1990, "Knapp is a must see for any Iowa Democrat seeking high office, not to mention presidential candidates who come here for the Iowa caucuses."[4]

Hughes saw Bill as a "good guy": "If he knows the right thing to do, he'll do it. He's a tough guy, and a hard guy, but a soft-hearted guy." Hughes soon tapped into this compassion, taking Bill on a tour of the most destitute neighborhoods of Des Moines, those mired in persistent poverty. Bill readily acknowledged Hughes's role in showing him the inequities of society and encouraging him to help those in need. "Harold broadened my outlook. He made me more focused. He helped me care more for people who don't have much because early in his governorship we worked with the inner city. . . . Harold got me interested in that arena."[5]

For example, Governor Hughes named Bill, John Grubb, and other Iowa business leaders to a state committee focused on low-income housing. At the time, the Des Moines area council of churches was pushing for an urban renewal housing project in the Oakridge neighborhood northwest of downtown. The project faced several hurdles, but the major one resulted from the sluggishness of the Federal Housing Authority in providing the low-interest loans needed before construction could begin. Hughes led a delegation that included Bill, Grubb, banker Dick Bryan, and others to Washington, D.C., to describe Iowa's urban renewal issues and get the FHA money freed up. The group met with officials from the Department of Housing and Urban Development, but the high point of the trip was a ten-minute private meeting with President Lyndon Johnson, which became a forty-five-minute discussion.[6]

The trip proved successful, and the FHA loans soon came through, allowing the Homes of Oakridge, the city's first and largest low-income housing project, to go up. Opening in 1969, it was the beginning of Bill's involvement in improving downtown Des Moines and helping the impoverished. His efforts in both these areas would pick up dramatically over the next few decades. He became a major supporter and fundraiser for such organizations as Tiny Tots Childcare Center, the Door of Faith Mission, Des Moines's Bethel Mission, the Homes of Oakridge, and Meals from the Heartland. And he would lead the revitalization of the Drake neighborhood in the 1980s.[7]

Meanwhile, the close relationship the two enjoyed soon spawned gossip that Hughes had leaked detailed information to Bill about planned interstate routes through the state, allowing him to buy acres of land cheaply at proposed entrance and exit ramps ahead of construction. Such land would jump in value when the highway was completed. Iowa

Realty did purchase land along the interstate routes, but no evidence ever surfaced to support these allegations of misconduct.[8]

Both Bill and Hughes firmly denied any wrongdoing. Bill explained that his purchases were based on public information. He added, "We bought a lot of land at proposed highway exits, but you only hear about where we were successful. No one talks about the land we acquired in Truro, for example, which we bought as farmland and sold as farmland at no profit." Eventually these rumors died down, but soon another rumor circulated about the popular politician.[9]

By late 1969, near the end of his first year in the U.S. Senate, Hughes's magnetic personality and commanding presence had captivated many, and he began to be discussed as a possible dark horse candidate in the upcoming presidential election. Hughes was merely flattered at first, but he then considered the idea seriously and set up an office in Washington, D.C., to explore his chances. Bill was delighted: "He was one of the great people in politics. The sky was the limit for Harold. He was a natural born leader."[10]

In early 1971, Bill set up a Hughes for President office in downtown Des Moines to raise money for the candidate. He hired Connie Wimer to run it. Many central Iowans thought highly of Hughes, and money began pouring into the office. But Hughes soon felt uncomfortable in situations where he thought he had to compromise his ideals to win people's support, and he even went out of his way to express opinions he knew would not be well received. Such positions hurt his campaign effort, which was further damaged when Hughes's belief in clairvoyance and mental telepathy came out. "The ball game was over," Bill knew, when the *Des Moines Register* reported that Hughes attended séances where he communicated with his dead brother. The senator withdrew from the race in July 1971.[11]

Bill was angry and disappointed with Hughes, who, he believed, "had so much potential and just threw it away." He felt the same way three years later, when the senator chose to step down and dedicate himself to the lay ministry by establishing alcohol treatment centers in Maryland. But after several years, Hughes found himself struggling financially, and

Bill convinced him to return to Iowa in the spring of 1981, creating a flexible counseling job for him at Iowa Realty that allowed the former senator plenty of time to continue his ministry.[12]

But Bill had also been quietly urging Hughes to return to politics and run for governor of Iowa in 1982. Hughes did not come back to the state to seek the office, but he began thinking about it. By the fall, Hughes appeared ready to run, but he encountered a problem with the Iowa residency requirement, which required gubernatorial candidates to have resided in the state two years prior to the election.[13]

That December Mary Jane Odell, Iowa's secretary of state and its top election official, ruled that Hughes had not met the residency requirement to run for governor. Much to Bill's chagrin, Hughes chose not to contest the decision, and he announced that he was bowing out of the race.[14]

Several years later, Hughes moved to Arizona, where he died in 1996. After he left Iowa, Bill explained, "We just sort of went our separate ways. I don't think he liked that. He would rather have had us stay closer together, and I would have too. But it was just hard—hard for us to go down that same path again."[15]

Although Bill lost touch with Hughes, the senator's lasting influence on him was undeniable. Hughes had altered Bill's life trajectory, getting him much more involved in Democratic politics and opening his eyes to the needs of the less fortunate in Des Moines and central Iowa.

JOHN RUAN

Chapter Nineteen

Bill Knapp and John Ruan at the Iowa State Fair, 2000.
Courtesy of Susan Knapp.

John Ruan, the prominent Des Moines business leader who had built his fortune in the trucking industry, was largely responsible for bringing Bill "into the downtown business fraternity" and involving him in rebuilding the city center. The process began when Ruan asked Bill to join the board of Bankers Trust, his downtown-based bank. Bill accepted the position in 1973.[1]

Some may have thought Ruan's move odd. Bill was twelve years younger than the trucker and a leading Democrat, while Ruan was one of the state's top Republican fundraisers. Yet Ruan probably saw much of himself in the younger businessman. Both were self-made, both were known to be determined and forceful, and both had risen rapidly in their respective fields. Bill, meanwhile, looked up to Ruan because "he thought big, did big things, and took risks." In fact, the two had become good friends in the 1960s, most likely because of their shared connection to lawyer and businessman Joe Rosenfield, a close friend and mentor to both.[2]

The following year, Ruan further enmeshed Bill with downtown business leadership. After he was elected president of the Greater Des Moines Committee, Ruan invited Bill to join the select group. Founded in 1907 as an association of past presidents of the city's chamber of commerce, the GDMC had evolved into an exclusive group of the city's foremost business figures that met once a week to discuss Des Moines's pressing economic issues. Ruan knew Bill was a doer and a pusher, and he thought this aggressiveness was just what the GDMC and downtown needed.[3]

These two positions allowed Bill to get acquainted with important business leaders and reconnect with others. It also gave him an insider's view of the early stages of the downtown renaissance. As Bill had noted, by the late 1960s "downtown was really kind of a disaster." Retailers had fled for the suburbs, soon followed by businesses and offices. This left downtown with dilapidated buildings and empty structures. But there were also hints of a turnaround toward the end of the decade: a new federal office building as well as the United Central Bank tower. These were followed in 1971 with the completion of a new Employers Mutual home office and a new J. C. Penney store. Several years later, big changes came with the construction of two skyscrapers, the twenty-five-story Financial Center and John Ruan's thirty-six-story Ruan Center, which became the tallest building in the state until the forty-five-story 801 Grand, the Principal Financial tower, dethroned it in 1990.[4]

Bill watched all this activity with great interest but was not yet involved downtown. Other projects occupied his time, and some included Ruan as well. For instance, he, Ruan, and Rosenfield tried to take over Merle Hay Mall (formerly Merle Hay Plaza) in 1976. Together, they offered $1.5 million for a 35 percent ownership stake, and if successful they had an agreement to combine their share with that of a Los Angeles attorney who owned 15 percent, which would give the four control of the property. But their effort fell short, and because they were not interested in being minority shareholders, the three dropped their plans and walked away.[5]

Later that decade, Bill and Ruan partnered again on another deal outside the city's downtown when the two bought the Blair House apartments in Cedar Rapids and converted them to condominiums. By that time, however, it was obvious that Ruan's focus remained, and Bill's focus had become, downtown Des Moines.[6]

Not surprisingly, a year after his 1977 purchase of the Hotel Savery, Bill's involvement in downtown picked up. In 1978, he and associates from the Greater Des Moines Committee joined the reconfigured Des Moines Development Corporation, a nonprofit affiliate of the Greater Des Moines Chamber of Commerce. Intended to bring economic development to downtown Des Moines, the group was reserved for CEOs who could make decisions quickly and could afford the high annual dues. The small membership was a who's who of the city's business community. Besides Bill and Ruan it included, for instance, David Kruidenier, CEO of the Des Moines Register and Tribune Company; Robert Burnett, president of the Meredith Corporation; John Fitzgibbon, president of Iowa–Des Moines National Bank (now Wells Fargo); James Hubbell Jr., head of Equitable of Iowa (now Voya Financial); and Bob Houser, CEO of Bankers Life (now the Principal Financial Group). Houser volunteered as the group's president.[7]

Bill quickly became one of the most active members of the Des Moines Development Corporation. If Ruan had kickstarted the downtown revival with his Ruan Center, his smaller Two Ruan Center office building next door, the thirty-three-story Marriott Hotel, and the beginnings of the climate-controlled skywalk system, Bill kept the business district's rehabilitation going. He brought in new members to the DMDC, promoted additional downtown projects, and put together deals that made them possible.

It was Bill who led the way with the DMDC's first major effort, buying up the old buildings on the so-called Ward Block west of the area now known as Cowles Commons to make the land available for development. The area also sat directly across Locust Street from Bill's Hotel Savery, giving him a real incentive to see its redevelopment take place rapidly. Here he arranged quite a few deals and acquired the block's various properties on the DMDC's behalf. The city then put the land up for bids and sought proposals for development.[8]

The Chicago firm Draper and Kramer edged out the competition with an eight-story structure featuring a large atrium in the center. But before the company could obtain the financing to begin construction, it needed to line up major tenants. Bill helped here as well, persuading United Federal Savings and Loan (which became part of US Bank) and Kirke–Van Orsdel Insurance Services (later acquired by Marsh and McLennan) to sign on as its first major tenants. Construction began, and the new Capital Square office building was completed in 1983. Bill was pleased with the new view to the south of the Hotel Savery, noting that the "downtown showplace" replaced the "drab and dreary" structures of before.[9]

He also played a primary role in bringing affordable housing to downtown, first with Elsie Mason Manor, a high-rise apartment facility for the elderly, in 1981, which Des Moines Mayor Pete Crivaro called "the crown jewel of downtown development." Even as this was going up, Bill was working on more housing. He put together a consortium of twenty-six local companies to build Civic Center Court, a 140-unit garden apartment complex designed for people who worked downtown. It opened the next year. These were followed by yet another project that, like Ruan Center, altered the city's skyline. Acting on behalf of the Des Moines Development Corporation, Bill acquired land for a much desired high-rise luxury condominium project. He then lured Minneapolis developer Ted Glasrud to Des Moines to build the Plaza condominium tower, which opened to much fanfare in 1985.[10]

Bob Houser was impressed with Bill's role in the downtown renaissance of the 1970s and 1980s: "As much as anybody and more than most, Bill Knapp has been a key factor in the success of Des Moines development." Unfortunately, Houser would not live to see Bill participate in the next round of downtown renewal. In 2012 Larry Zimpleman, then CEO of the Principal Financial Group, became a leading advocate for a new version of the DMDC. Soon other heavyweights, including Steve Lacy, then CEO of Meredith, Jim Cownie, a former cable executive and a good friend of Bill's, and Gene Meyer, president of the Greater Des Moines Partnership, backed the idea. Bill embraced the plan as well and soon recruited friends and colleagues to be part of the new nonprofit. Ultimately, he and seventeen other business leaders and companies joined the new Des Moines Redevelopment Corporation.[11]

True to form, Bill was again right in the middle of the activity, discussing proposals, negotiating land swaps, and making purchases for the Des Moines Redevelopment Corporation, all to clear the path for new development. After a series of complex deals, new projects began sprouting across downtown. These included the new YMCA, located in the former Polk County Convention Complex; the new Polk County Courthouse Annex, situated in the former J. C. Penney Building; the new Hilton Hotel, just southwest of the Iowa Events Center; and plans for a new federal courthouse where the old Riverfront YMCA had stood.[12]

Years earlier, Ruan bucked the advice of a handful of business associates and brought his friend Bill Knapp onto the Des Moines Development Corporation. As he recalled, "Because of Bill's aggressiveness, some of the people downtown didn't want him on the Greater Des Moines Committee. But I put him on anyway." The move was propitious. It dialed Bill into the needs of downtown, where he made things happen with much of his work, whether he was negotiating for land, finding developers, or securing tenants, all done without the benefit of commissions. Of course, Bill's activity was not entirely selfless, and he benefited from a revitalized downtown, which increased area property values. More specifically, he saw opportunity here where others did not, and with his purchase of the rundown Hotel Savery, Bill took advantage of what he thought could become the hot spot in the up-and-coming downtown.[13]

GUIDO FENU

Chapter Twenty

Bill Knapp and Guido Fenu at Bill's seventy-fifth birthday party, 2001. Courtesy of Jo Fenu.

Many, including Bill's brother, Paul, were certain he had made a mistake when he bought the rundown Hotel Savery in 1977. Conventional wisdom held that the old downtown hotels such as the Savery or the Fort Des Moines would be badly hurt by competition from the new hotels being considered. Ruan's modern downtown Marriott Hotel skyscraper, which grew out of these plans, was located a few blocks to the west of Bill's recent purchase. "There were people," Bill recalled, "who thought I'd met my Waterloo." Indeed, the acquisition was a gamble, but it proved a triumph, due in no small part to Bill's partnership with locally renowned restaurateur Guido Fenu. In fact, Bill explained, "We would not have been successful at the Savery without Guido. He did a hell of a job for us."[1]

Fenu was born in Sardinia, a large Italian island in the Mediterranean Sea, and learned the restaurant and hotel business in Berlin before working as a headwaiter and maître d' in fine restaurants in Italy, France, Switzerland, and England. In 1960, the twenty-one-year-old immigrated to New York City, and by 1965 Fenu was providing the food service on a cruise ship based out of Ft. Lauderdale. He learned of Des Moines while on this ship.[2]

Des Moines resident F. A. Wittern Sr., the founder of Fawn Engineering, a designer of vending machines, was on the cruise. Impressed with Fenu, he told him he should come to Des Moines. When Wittern returned home, he begged Johnny Compiano, the owner of the popular Johnny and Kay's Restaurant on Fleur Drive, to hire Fenu. Compiano complied, offered Fenu a job, and sent him a round-trip ticket to Des Moines. Fenu started at the restaurant in 1965. He worked there several years, then moved on to the Des Moines Golf and Country Club before starting his own catering business in 1972.[3]

Six years later, he returned to Fleur Drive with his own eatery, Guido's Restaurant and Lounge, situated across from the Des Moines International Airport. The Grumpy Gourmet, the *Des Moines Tribune*'s food critic, visited the establishment six days after it opened and reported that it had "class and style," the same characteristics that had "long distinguished Guido Fenu's Catering Service." The reviewer concluded with high praise: "I believe it will be one of the top eating places in the city. I am sure Guido intends to do everything he can to make it so."[4]

Meanwhile, Bill had begun what would be a $7 million facelift of his downtown hotel. Iowa Realty's in-house architect and designer, Don Bemis, oversaw the work, which was done by remodeling experts Bloodgood and Associates and the realty firm's own Midland Builders. As the rehabilitation began, Bill looked for someone to run the hotel's food service. This would include an upscale restaurant and bar in the space where the Bohemian Club had been located (the club moved to the Hotel Fort Des Moines and later Capital Square before merging with the Embassy Club), a revamped coffee shop, and the hotel's convention catering business.[5]

Bill's search for a restaurateur to oversee the hotel's food operation did not take long: he soon zeroed in on Fenu. He knew of Fenu's work at Johnny and Kay's as well as his catering business and restaurant. Certain that Fenu's reputation would draw people to the Savery, Bill offered him a fifty-fifty partnership in the hotel's food service, with the two splitting the profits equally. The deal also gave Fenu a much larger, more prominent space to showcase his talents, and he jumped at the opportunity.[6]

The hotel's coffee shop was renamed the Sidewalk Café and opened in late 1979, but everyone was waiting for Guido's Restaurant and, to a lesser extent, Guido's Lounge, both of which opened in March 1980. Just as Bill had expected, Fenu served exceptional food and wine with his signature flair and style, and beginning that November the cool jazz sounds of the popular singer and pianist Irene Myles and her group wafted from the lounge.[7]

Fenu was at the restaurant and lounge "all the time," Bill recalled, and according to the *Register*, "people say Guido's personal attention lends it the dimension of a private club—without the dues." The chic spot was soon considered the area's top restaurant, and the lounge became the city's place to see and be seen.[8]

Gene Moore, the Savery's manager, later noted that although the Knapp-owned hotel initially operated in the red, "it always made money, starting in 1980." While true, what Moore did not highlight was the importance of Fenu and the food business to the hotel's bottom line. Bill Knapp II clarified, "We split the food service profits fifty-fifty with Guido, and we were making more money from our half of those profits than from the hotel's rooms for darn near the entire time we worked with him. We were doing well, and Guido was doing well. It could not have been any better."[9]

Fenu excelled at all aspects of the food business; according to the *Register*, he "set the standard for all fine dining in the state." Bill, however, knew he could be stubborn and persnickety. He recalled, "I got along with Guido fine," but the same could not be said for Carole Baumgarten, the hotel manager who followed Moore in 1991. Clashes between the two grew in frequency until the spring of 1993, when Fenu decided to pull the plug, end the joint venture, and close Guido's after thirteen years. Three years later, Bill sold the Savery for $7.45 million as part of his move to get out of the hotel and restaurant business. Fenu, meanwhile, went on to open the restaurant at Glen Oaks Country Club in West Des Moines, then operated several other eateries in the area before retiring to Santa Barbara in 2005. He died eight years later.[10]

"I loved the Savery and all the excitement around the place," Bill fondly remembered, "and I especially loved visiting with VIPs in town who frequently stopped in the restaurant and bar. Guido did a great job and was instrumental to our success there. He was one of the best restaurateurs in the country and added a real pizzazz to our hotel. Everyone wanted to go to Guido's."[11]

ED CAMPBELL AND BONNIE CAMPBELL

Chapter Twenty-One

Ed Campbell, circa 1982.
Courtesy of Bonnie Campbell.

Bonnie Campbell, circa 1991.
Courtesy of Bonnie Campbell.

While Bill owned the Savery, he developed an especially close relationship with Ed and Bonnie Campbell, a prominent couple in Iowa Democratic circles. The Campbells became hugely important to Bill politically, professionally, and personally, and not surprisingly the three spent an inordinate amount of time together at Guido's throughout the 1980s and into the early 1990s. "We were like family," Bonnie recalled.[1]

Bill met both through Harold Hughes. A graduate of the University of Iowa, Ed began his career working for the chambers of commerce in Grinnell and Charles City before joining Hughes's gubernatorial staff as a special assistant in 1965. It was here that Bill became acquainted with him; as Ed explained, "We sort of gravitated to each other—chemistry, I guess." The two became good friends and remained so when Ed went with Hughes to Washington, D.C., after the governor was elected to the U.S. Senate in 1968. Bill, in fact, went with Hughes, Ed, and the rest of the staff to help them find housing in the nation's capital.[2]

While on the senator's staff, Ed met his wife-to-be, Bonnie Pierce. Bonnie was born in upstate New York and raised on a modest dairy farm. After graduating from high school in 1965, she went to Washington, D.C., as part of a federal antipoverty program. There she worked as a clerk for Robert Weaver, head of the Department of Housing and Urban Development, for two years before taking a clerical position on a Senate subcommittee on intergovernmental relations chaired by Senator Edward Muskie. In March 1969, she joined Hughes's staff, charged with assisting Iowans who needed help navigating the federal bureaucracy.[3]

Ed had been invaluable to Hughes, who said he was "as good an assistant as I've ever seen." The *Des Moines Tribune* was more specific, saying that Ed had been Hughes's "man for all seasons," serving as his "scheduler, political organizer, coat carrier, confidant, and troubleshooter." When Hughes decided to retire from the Senate after one term, Ed returned to Iowa to run Congressman John Culver's successful 1974 campaign for the Senate seat. He and Bonnie married that December, and they stayed in Iowa, where Ed oversaw Culver's state offices for the next two years. After mounting an unsuccessful effort for a state Senate seat, Ed began selling real estate for Iowa Realty and was elected chair of the Iowa Democratic Party, where he would serve until 1982.[4]

Because Bill had seen just how helpful Ed had been for Hughes, he hired his friend and political strategist as his personal assistant in 1979. Ed set up shop in the office next to Bill's and became his right-hand man, handling both political and business matters. His experience navigating government bureaucracy proved essential in securing the necessary federal funding for Elsie Mason Manor, the downtown housing project Bill had promoted. Likewise, his background working with various constituencies was helpful when he assisted Bill in his effort to expand the city's skywalk system.[5]

Then, in a familiar political role, he and Bill encouraged Senator Hughes to return to politics and run for governor in the 1982 election. But when Hughes's campaign was derailed by the state's residency requirement, the senator and Bill urged Campbell, who had earlier considered seeking the office, to run. He did, but the effort was problematic from the start, as Ed was largely viewed as a behind-the-scenes political fixer. Worse, he was seen by many as "Bill Knapp's candidate for governor." Unfortunately, one of Bill's fundraising tactics only seemed to confirm the suspicion when he sent a letter to Iowa Realty employees soliciting donations for Ed's campaign. Some at the firm felt uncomfortable about the pressure to support Ed and gave a copy of the letter to the *Des Moines Register*, which publicly rebuked Bill for the "arm-twisting" move.[6]

Clearly, Bill's loyalty to Ed had trumped his good sense, and despite all Bill's support Ed came in a distant third in the Democratic primary that June, which was won by former U.S. attorney Roxanne Conlin. She ultimately lost in November to Republican Terry Branstad. After the loss, Ed remained with Bill for a couple more years before starting his own lobbying business. Bill and Iowa Realty were his first clients.[7]

Bonnie, meanwhile, worked for John Culver as a field office coordinator in Iowa from late 1974 through 1980. Toward the end of her time with the senator, she began taking classes at Des Moines Area Community College. After Culver lost his seat to Chuck Grassley in 1980, Bonnie became an agent at Iowa Realty and sold homes part-time while earning her bachelor's degree at Drake University in 1982. Three years later, she completed law school at Drake as well. She clerked and then went to work for the Wimer law firm, but she left for the Belin firm with Tom Flynn and Gerry Neugent in 1989, after Bill Knapp moved Iowa Realty's business away from the Wimer firm.[8]

But politics was her first love. Bonnie served as the chair of the Iowa Democratic Party from 1987 until 1991 and was elected Iowa's attorney general in 1990. She then ran unsuccessfully for governor in 1994. The following spring, President Bill Clinton appointed her director of the Office on Violence Against Women of the U.S. Department of Justice. Bonnie had long been an advocate of legal reform in cases of domestic violence and abuse. She remained in that position until 2001 and stayed in the capital at a Washington, D.C., law firm before returning to Iowa to practice law in 2003.[9]

Years earlier, in the 1970s, Bill and the Campbells began socializing together and grew close. Hours of conversation and friendly arguments with the two helped shape and sharpen Bill's views and understanding of politics. He, Ed, and Bonnie regularly met for dinner on Saturday nights, sometimes joined by businessmen and prominent Democrats Joe Rosenfield and John Chrystal as well. Ed and Bonnie frequently got together with Bill Knapp and Connie Wimer years before their affair was widely known. The couples usually visited at Bill's Timberline property, the acreage he used for entertaining in what is now Urbandale. Ed and Bonnie even became Bill's next-door neighbors at the Plaza condominiums in the late 1980s, and they later built a house near Bill's in Iowa Realty's Napa Valley development.[10]

Bill, Ed, and Bonnie also vacationed together, but one trip stood out in Bonnie's mind. During a particularly miserable stretch of winter in the late 1970s, Bill was eager to get out of the cold for a few days, so he, brother Paul, the Campbells, and Bill and Connie Wimer went to the exclusive Fontainebleau Hotel in Miami. At dinner the last evening of their stay, Bill told everyone that he had had an especially good time, and he was picking up the tab for the entire trip. Bonnie was flabbergasted and remembered thinking, "I'd have to mortgage my house to treat the group to all this, but Bill was generous like that."[11]

The Campbells became and remained important mainstays in Bill's inner circle. They were "damn good friends," Bill remembered, until Ed finally lost his long battle with cancer and died in 2010. Bonnie Campbell continues to be one of Bill's oldest and dearest friends. In 2018, she married Mark Hamilton, owner of Times-Citizen Communications, a media company that publishes the *Iowa Falls Times Citizen* and the *Ackley*

World Journal. Bonnie and Hamilton met years earlier when they both served on Harold Hughes's staff in Washington, D.C., and interestingly, it was Ed Campbell who hired him for the job.[12]

DWAYNE McANINCH

Chapter Twenty-Two

Dwayne McAninch, 2007. Courtesy of the McAninch Corporation.

In the summer of 2006, Des Moines entrepreneur Gary Kirke threw a party for two of his friends, Bill Knapp and earthmoving contractor Dwayne McAninch, who shared a July 18 birthday (Bill turned eighty that year, McAninch seventy). The festivities were originally scheduled for Kirke's Fratello's restaurant in West Des Moines, but when the guest list approached three hundred, he moved the party to his Jalapeño Pete's restaurant and bar at the Iowa State Fairgrounds. "I do an annual corn-fest party" every July, Kirke explained. Then, playing with the words "icon" and "corn," he added in jest that "this year I figured I'd honor two local business i-corns."[1]

Bill and McAninch were longtime friends who started doing business together in the mid-1960s. Like Bill, McAninch was raised on an Iowa farm, first in Carlisle and then in Norwalk, two small towns just south of Des Moines. Also like Bill, he did not like farm chores and hoped to avoid the life of a farmer. "Farming was so much work," he noted. "You had to milk those damn cows by hand, and they tied you down so tight." And like Bill, McAninch found his ticket off the farm. In his case, it was with earthmoving, and it was this that brought him into contact with Bill.[2]

McAninch's father, George, bought a small bulldozer in 1947 and started a side business digging ponds and doing other earthmoving work for fellow farmers. Young McAninch was intrigued by the bulldozer and immediately liked driving it more than the family tractor. Soon he joined his father in the small earthmoving operation. By 1954, the eighteen-year-old thought the bulldozer could be the basis of a successful business, and he bought it from his father and set out on his own.[3]

He continued with small jobs digging ponds or terracing fields until he landed a sizable contract in Norwalk. There developer Lloyd Clark was planning to build the Lakewood residential community around the to-be-constructed 170-acre Lake Colchester. McAninch was hired to dig the lake in 1965. That proved to be the "springboard for the business," Doug McAninch, Dwayne's son and now the president and CEO of the McAninch Corporation, recalled. "The job moved Dad from farm work to bigger jobs and got him into the Des Moines market." That same year, Dwayne McAninch met Bill Knapp when he hired McAninch to do the grading and ground preparation for a warehouse he was constructing on Des Moines's south side.[4]

McAninch remembered his initial impression of Bill. "He was a smart, serious, and successful guy, and his big blue Cadillac told me he had made it." Meanwhile, McAninch was on his way to making it as well. The Norwalk job indeed led to others; he added equipment and personnel; and he incorporated the firm in 1967. Bill and Iowa Realty continued using McAninch as one of several earthmoving companies they hired, especially for the apartments they were putting up, and over time they relied more and more heavily on the McAninch Corporation. Besides being reliable, Bill recalled, the company was more efficient than the competition. He once told Dwayne, "You always charged me more per hour, but at the end of the day, your bill was always less."[5]

The firm thus won Bill's respect, and by the mid-1970s he began using it almost exclusively for his grading and utility work. The bigger jobs McAninch completed for Bill and Iowa Realty or, later, Knapp Properties included the developments of Adventureland Estates, Napa Valley, Country Club business park, Westchester Manor, Interstate Acres, West Lakes, Airport Commerce Park, the Tournament Club of Iowa, and Prairie Crossing.[6]

Bill was more than just a big and consistent customer of Dwayne's: "I've learned a lot from working with Bill Knapp . . . how to control costs, how to get things done quickly, and how important it is to get things done on time and on budget." Moreover, when the McAninch Corporation lost millions in the oil pipeline business when the price of oil fell by 70 percent in the early 1980s, Bill helped Dwayne put together a plan to sell equipment, which kept the company from serious financial trouble.[7]

Whenever Dwayne and his firm had the opportunity to return the favor, they did. Such was the case in 1990, when Bill sold fifteen prime acres on University Avenue just north of the Des Moines Golf and Country Club in Clive to developer Ken Smith for $1 million. The agreement came with Bill's promise that 142nd Street, then a gravel road on the western edge of the acreage, would be paved from University Avenue north to Hickman Road within a year. Unfortunately, the economy had dipped into a recession, and Smith began to reconsider his purchase. If the one-year paving deadline were not met, Smith could and likely would back out of the agreement.[8]

As usual, Bill had retained McAninch for the work. But the road to be paved divided the suburbs of Clive and Waukee, and the cities bickered over how to pay for the improvements. Waukee refused to put money into the project. Clive eventually issued bonds to cover the Waukee side of the road, and Iowa Realty bought the bonds, which would be paid for by future property taxes from the eventual residents in the development. This plus bad weather slowed the roadwork considerably, and it looked like Smith could extricate himself from the deal when the time limit for paving expired. Bill called Dwayne and asked McAninch to make this job its top priority. "We did," Doug McAninch remembered. "We knew we had to get it done and pulled some rabbits out of hats to do it." Bill was relieved when McAninch met the deadline, and Smith closed on the deal.[9]

That was not all the magic up McAninch's sleeve. In 1999, Dwayne took a big technological leap forward when, working with Caterpillar, the heavy equipment manufacturer, and Trimble, a maker of navigation systems, he became the first earthmoving contractor in the country to introduce global positioning systems in his equipment. The advance was revolutionary. "It saves money and it saves time," Dwayne said of his introduction of GPS. "Jobs are done in half the time and they are safer." Bill II remembered being impressed. "With GPS, McAninch didn't need engineers to stake the projects. The grading was more precise, and the jobs were completed faster."[10]

Besides their close business connection, Bill and Dwayne shared an interest in Democratic politics and philanthropy. Dwayne gave generously to many of Bill's political candidates and their campaigns. One of the first was Ed Campbell's gubernatorial run in 1982. But more importantly, Bill and Dwayne worked together on many philanthropic projects. The two joined forces, for example, and worked with others on the restoration of Des Moines's Gray's Lake Park. They were also both involved in the rebuilding of the Iowa State Fairgrounds. Besides giving generously to rebuild the historic grounds, Dwayne donated the grading and site preparation for the construction of the fair's Paul R. Knapp Animal Learning Center, completed in 2007. That same year, when the fair had started to consider a new indoor arena, he, Bill, John Putney, head of the Iowa State Fair's fundraising arm, the Blue Ribbon Foundation, fair manager Gary Slater, and several others flew down to Texas and Oklahoma on Dwayne's private jet to see similar facilities at the Amarillo National Center and the Tulsa State Fairgrounds. This trip provided several ideas for the Iowa State Fair and ultimately resulted in the erection of the Richard O. Jacobson Exhibition Center in 2010.[11]

As Doug explained, "Whenever Bill called [asking us to support a cause], my dad knew he had skin in the game, so Dad gave generously. Likewise, we could call Bill for causes we supported, and he always opened his wallet for us."[12]

The friendship, however, was built on a highly successful business relationship. Bill said of Dwayne, "He is the most honorable businessman I know. He was instrumental in all our developments because we could count on him to have the work done fast and done right. His pioneering use of GPS only made McAninch that much better."[13]

DAVID KRUIDENIER

Chapter Twenty-Three

David Kruidenier, circa 1995. Courtesy of Bill Knapp.

Remarkably, Bill also shared his July 18 birthday with David Kruidenier—another close friend and civic leader in Des Moines. It was a most improbable friendship, however, because the birthday seemed to be the only thing the two had in common. Unlike the self-made real estate magnate, Kruidenier was born into wealth and influence. Five years older than Bill, he was a third-generation member of Des Moines's prominent Cowles media family, which had owned and operated the

Des Moines Register and *Tribune* since 1903 and the *Minneapolis Star Tribune* since the 1930s.

After starting his education in Des Moines's public schools, Kruidenier graduated from the elite Phillips Exeter Academy in New Hampshire before heading to the Ivy League, where he received a bachelor's degree from Yale and then a master's in business administration from Harvard. He began his career at the family's Minneapolis newspaper in 1948, the same year he married Elizabeth Woodwell Stuart. Liz eventually became an attorney and a prominent community leader as well.[1]

Kruidenier moved back to Des Moines in 1952, where he joined the Des Moines Register and Tribune Company as the assistant business manager. Thus began his thirty-three-year career at his family's papers, and he moved up the ladder until he was named president and publisher in 1971. Once Kruidenier was back in the city, he and Bill eventually became aware of each other, but they ran in very different social circles. And even though the two met through Bill and Connie Wimer, they did not initially become friends, as Liz Kruidenier explained, because they were so different: "David's an aesthete, and Bill is very practical and doesn't share David's interest in art, architecture, or literature."[2]

Moreover, as the publisher of the *Register* and *Tribune*, Kruidenier was especially careful to avoid relationships that could be construed as a conflict of interest even though he maintained a hands-off policy when it came to the selection of news stories or their placement in the paper. "David played that to the Nth degree," Bill remembered. "You know, he would hold anybody at arm's length, not only me but anyone else." Regardless, Kruidenier sometimes faced criticism from business leaders who complained when the papers took what they considered to be antibusiness stands. But he held firm and supported his editors' decisions. "To do our job responsibly often irritates people.... I doubt if I have a single good friend who hasn't been upset or irritated by something in the newspaper. At times it makes me uncomfortable in social situations. At times it makes things difficult."[3]

All this changed when the Cowles family sold the Register and Tribune Company to Gannett in 1985, and for the first time in decades

Kruidenier felt free to spend time with whomever he pleased. Over the next few years, he cultivated several new friendships, but the most unlikely was the close bond he developed with Bill Knapp. Bill recalls, "David and I were as opposite as two people can be, but I respected him and liked him a lot. We enjoyed being around each other and became great friends."[4]

Ultimately, the two realized that they shared some key characteristics. Besides the common birthday, both were astute and bright and cared deeply for the city of Des Moines. They also soon found that they enjoyed teasing each other at every opportunity. "He was kind of caustic," Bill noted, "but I'd be caustic right back." Liz Kruidenier described the relationship: "For Bill," she observed, "David represented approval of the establishment, and he was someone Bill could go to for advice. David was drawn to Bill's quick mind and his unpolished outrageousness."[5]

Previously, Bill and Kruidenier had been in different camps when it came to downtown development in the 1970s and early 1980s. Kruidenier was a major backer of the Civic Center, which Bill had originally opposed. Later, Bill supported John Ruan's Marriott Hotel plan while Kruidenier did not. But any rancor from these disagreements fell by the wayside when the two became close friends in the late 1980s.[6]

Soon they began traveling together. Bill Knapp and Connie Wimer had remained together after Bill and Irene divorced in 1987, and the two flew to Egypt with the Kruideniers for a Nile River cruise in 1990. The following year, they joined the Kruideniers and others in England for an elegant seventieth birthday party that Liz organized for David. The lavish soiree was held at Cliveden House, a luxury manor twenty-five miles northwest of London. Other trips followed after Bill and Connie split up, with Bill and Susan Terry (now Knapp) traveling with the Kruideniers many times, including a trip to France and an Alaskan cruise.[7]

During their many trips together, Kruidenier tried to broaden Bill's outlook and schooled him in the history, art, and architecture of the many places they visited, but Bill was not that interested. "I've seen a lot of cathedrals and stuff like that," he remarks, "but I'm just not anxious to see such things again."[8]

But they did share an important idea after the trip to London for David's party, when the two decided to celebrate their July 18 birthdays together. These gatherings were generally noteworthy, bringing together civic, business, and political leaders from the greater Des Moines community, but the most memorable party took place in 2001. In honor of Bill's seventy-fifth birthday and David's eightieth, Susan Knapp arranged for singer Willie Nelson to perform. The party was held that July at Bill's River House just west of the Napa Valley development, where three hundred guests ate barbecue, danced, and enjoyed listening to the country music legend.[9]

Bill delighted in the parties, but it was the frequent conversations he shared with David that were particularly important to him. He often sought his older friend's counsel, especially when it came to philanthropy and civic activity. Kruidenier had been instilled with the idea of noblesse oblige, which held that the wealthy had a responsibility to give back to the community, and Bill had long admired the Cowles family's tradition of generous giving.[10]

By the time he and Kruidenier became friendly, Bill had already started making donations in greater Des Moines, largely to organizations that assisted the less fortunate in the downtown area. He soon recognized that such activity made him feel good, and Connie Wimer recalled, "The more he gave, the happier he became." By the early 1980s, Bill had taken his first steps to be more strategic in his philanthropy, creating the Iowa Realty Foundation for corporate giving in 1983 and the William C. Knapp Charitable Foundation for personal donations in 1985.[11]

But it was Kruidenier, Bill acknowledged, who "expanded my thinking about philanthropy and helped me understand that because I had done well, I had a social duty to give back to the community." This growing appreciation and Kruidenier's encouragement led Bill to make larger and more significant gifts across a broader array of nonprofits. Besides continuing to give to and raise money for downtown entities such as Des Moines's Bethel Mission, Tiny Tots Childcare Center, and the Homes of Oakridge, Bill took up additional causes. After leading the rehabilitation of the Drake University neighborhood in the mid-

1980s, he became even more involved with Drake University after son Roger became its tennis coach in 1989. He was soon cochairing (along with friends Jim Cownie and David Miller) the school's effort to raise funds for a new $12 million athletic arena. The three quickly had $6.7 million in hand, and then Bill donated $3 million to the effort. The building was completed in 1992 and, appropriately, was named the Knapp Center.[12]

It was as if this gift and activity on behalf of Drake primed the pump, and Bill took up philanthropy with the same exuberance he had for making deals. When Drake started another fundraising drive in the late 1990s, he gave $5 million to the effort; interestingly, his friends David and Liz Kruidenier contributed $5 million to the campaign as well.[13]

More large donations and fundraising work for other projects and institutions followed, making central Iowa a better place for all. Over the next fifteen years, Bill joined with David and Liz Kruidenier and others on the Gray's Lake Park rehabilitation and made leading gifts to organizations such as the Iowa State Fair, the Iowa Veterans Cemetery, Meals from the Heartland, and Iowa Methodist Medical Center (now part of Unity Point Health).[14]

Roughly a decade before Bill's gift to the medical center, his twenty-year friendship with David came to an end when the former publisher died in 2006. Bill missed his close friend and adviser, but his counsel and his advice to give back to the community stuck with Bill and live on through the real estate man's continuing largesse. In 2013, Bill channeled the thinking of his old friend when he explained, "If you have the means to do it, you owe a lot back. It's important that people know they have somewhat of an obligation to give back and do it as an example to others."[15]

ROGER BROOKS

Chapter Twenty-Four

Bill Knapp and Roger Brooks in Aspen, Colorado, 1992.
Courtesy of Bill Knapp.

Bill often used the sumptuous Christmas party he and Susan held every year to cut deals, but it was son-in-law Mark Haviland who worked on his behalf and arranged the deal of the evening at the 2018 gala. That summer, Bill had decided to get rid of his Rolls-Royce Wraith coupe because he enjoyed his four-door Rolls-Royce Ghost more, and the sportier model was getting little use. When he told Haviland that he wanted to sell the car, Haviland suggested that they could probably find a buyer among some of Bill's well-heeled friends. Bill liked the idea, and Haviland drew up a list of ten possibilities. The first two Haviland approached were not interested, but then he saw Roger Brooks, another person on the list and one of Bill's oldest friends, at the Knapps' holiday gathering and struck up a conversation.[1]

When Brooks, the retired CEO of AmerUs (the successor to Central Life Assurance, now part of Athene USA), heard about the Rolls-Royce, he was immediately intrigued. He remained so even after Haviland told him the auto was worth between $180,000 and $220,000. Brooks knew the car and had ridden in it; he offered Haviland $190,000 for it. Haviland went to ask Bill if Brooks's bid was adequate. "Hell, yes," he responded, "get the check." And that was what Haviland did; Brooks turned over an empty drink tray and wrote a check on the spot for $190,000. Bill was pleased but, compared to two pivotal deals he had done with Brooks in the 1980s, this one was minor.[2]

Like Bill, Brooks was also self-made. Born poor in Clarion, the Webster County seat ninety miles north of Des Moines, he was the tenth of eleven children. After graduating from his local high school, Brooks went to Drake University, in part because a friend got him a job at Dahl's Foods bagging groceries, which could help pay for his education. He later transferred to the University of Iowa when he was offered a scholarship, and he graduated with a degree in mathematics and plans to be an actuary. Brooks returned to Des Moines in 1959 and started a job at Central Life Assurance as an actuarial assistant.[3]

He advanced rapidly in the company, becoming vice president in 1968, president in 1972, and CEO two years later. It was in the early 1970s that Bill reached out and introduced himself to the insurance executive. "Bill always made sure he networked with anyone who might have clout someday," Brooks recalled, "and once I was named president, he saw me in that light." They became better friends in the late 1970s when Brooks joined the Breakfast Club, and the two discovered they shared a love of tennis. They began playing regularly, and as Brooks recalled, "we really bonded in one long-drawn-out singles match on a 103-degree summer day. Neither of us was willing to quit."[4]

As their friendship deepened, so too did the economic recession of the late 1970s. By the early 1980s, double-digit inflation and unemployment created difficult times for the real estate business. Amid this troubled market, Bill began looking for a partner with deep pockets to join Iowa Realty. He found one in Roger Brooks, who was then looking to expand and diversify Central Life. Bill raised the possibility while the two were playing tennis at his Timberline property in Urbandale. Central Life had already bought into real estate and development projects, largely in the Southwest, and Brooks was immediately interested.[5]

Negotiations ensued, and Central Life bought 80 percent of Iowa Realty in 1984. Bill, however, was given a free hand to run the operation as he saw fit, and he and his management team, headed up by brother Paul, were given employment contracts. Bill believed that with access to Central Life's capital, he could make more money by owning 20 percent of the company than he could when he had controlled all of it. Brooks seemed to share the feeling, "Making Bill Knapp an employee," he noted, "is a little like hitching a racehorse up to a plow."[6]

With Central Life providing financing at favorable rates, Bill began several new projects, including opening major subdivisions like Napa Valley, Country Club, and West Lakes, all in Des Moines's western suburbs. These pushed Iowa Realty to new heights and gave it an edge over its competitors. As Paul Knapp noted at the time, "Being a developer allows us to provide inventory to our agents." With more and more new homes available to sell, Iowa Realty increased the number of its agents by 20 percent, and its sales volume more than doubled over the next three years, rising from $169 million in 1985 to $341 million in 1988.[7]

Late that year, Brooks expressed interest in buying the rest of Iowa Realty, but the two partners were soon at loggerheads over the valuation of the remaining 20 percent. The earlier deal had valued Iowa Realty's goodwill at ten times its earnings, and this figure was to be used if Central Life wished to purchase the last portion of the company. But Iowa Realty's earnings grew much more rapidly than anyone had expected because of its access to Central Life's capital.[8]

During a highly contentious negotiation meeting in the spring of 1989, Bill and his colleagues at Iowa Realty and Central Life's team finally agreed on the real estate firm's future earnings estimate, but they were still far apart on its present value. Bill and his managers held to the valuation formula laid out in the 1984 deal, while Brooks and his associates argued that the ten times earnings figure should not be used because Iowa Realty's exceptional growth was fueled by financing from Central Life. Getting nowhere, both sides agreed to take a break.[9]

On his way back to the conference room to resume the meeting, Bill stopped by the office of Iowa Realty's trainer, Tim Meline, and picked up a rubber chicken, a prop Meline often used in his courses. Bill reentered the meeting with the rubber chicken, and without saying a word he grasped it by the neck and shook it in front of Brooks and his managers. All laughed, but Bill's message was clear: he had Central Life by the neck on the issue of valuing Iowa Realty stock. Brooks soon acquiesced, accepting Bill's position, and Central Life bought the outstanding shares of the firm for $7.99 million, 20 percent more than it had paid for the first 80 percent of the company five years earlier. As before, Bill and Iowa Realty's top executives signed contracts to stay in place for the next several years.[10]

The two deals proved to be big wins for Bill, and despite the rubber chicken episode, Brooks and AmerUs eventually came away winners as well. In 1998, Brooks sold Iowa Realty and his firm's majority stake in Edina Realty in Minnesota to MidAmerican Energy Holdings Company (now part of Berkshire Hathaway) for an estimated $75 to $100 million.[11]

But there was more to Bill's relationship with Brooks than business deals. The two grew to be close friends while both were struggling with their marriages, and they turned to each other for support. Outside of his brother, Paul, Bill saw Brooks as one of the few people he could talk to about family matters, Irene, or Connie Wimer. Brooks, likewise, viewed Bill as a confidant. Ultimately, each divorced—Bill in 1987 and Brooks the following year—but when each remarried, the other was there for his friend. Brooks went back to the altar in 1990, marrying Sunnie Richer in a small ceremony at the Aspen Chapel in Colorado. Bill served as his best man. Eight years later, Bill married Susan Terry at the same location, and Brooks and Richer stood up for the two.[12]

MIKE KNAPP

Chapter Twenty-Five

Mike Knapp, 2016. Courtesy of Iowa Realty.

By the time Roger Brooks bought most of Iowa Realty in 1984, it was becoming clear that Mike Knapp, Paul's oldest son, was the heir apparent to run the brokerage side of the business. Bill, in fact, had relied on family members from the start of Iowa Realty. Shortly after he took over the business from Byron Hollis in 1952, for example, he recruited Harold Knapp and Herman Miller to sell homes. Knapp was a cousin, the son of Bill's Uncle Floyd, while Miller was one of Floyd Knapp's sons-in-law. Both proved to be great salespeople. In the 1950s, Irene capably ran the firm's insurance operation and then handled the bookkeeping duties for two years. In 1956, Bill brought brother-in-law Clair Niday into the company, where he would be a mainstay for the next thirty years. A month after Niday started, Bill's brother, Paul, joined Iowa Realty.[1]

Bill always felt he could trust and rely on family members a little more than others, and the success of these hires only reinforced that notion. He was therefore happy when Mike, the first of the next generation of Knapps, started at Iowa Realty in the early 1970s. Mike had grown up around the business but had not intended to work there. However, while studying marketing at the University of Iowa, he decided to get his real estate license, and when he graduated in 1972 he asked his father for a job. That spring, Mike began at Iowa Realty as a residential sales agent, working out of the Beaver Avenue office.[2]

Over the next few years, Mike became one of the company's top salespeople, but he soon moved over to management. In 1980 Niday, then manager of the Beaver Avenue office, was promoted to general sales manager of the company. Until then, Vice President Paul Knapp had served in that capacity as well, but shedding the day-to-day duties of running the business freed Paul up to focus on longer-term strategy. Mike took over as the manager of the Beaver office.[3]

The job was an apprenticeship of sorts, a training ground for Mike, who was being groomed to take over as Iowa Realty's general manager. Four years later he did just that, when Niday prepared to retire and was named to the largely honorific job of director of operations. The move made Mike his father's right-hand man at the company, and it took place at a time of transition, shortly before Central Life Assurance bought 80 percent of the firm.[4]

As his father had done for years, Mike greased the wheels and kept the brokerage business humming along. Bill felt the business was in good hands; now armed with Central Life's capital, he pursued big deals and lined up big developments. The four hundred–acre Country Club project in Clive was the biggest, and Mike oversaw its sales and marketing. He noted that interest in the subdivision was "tremendous" when it opened, and a week after the first plat's seventy lots went up for sale in July 1988, they had all sold. Kelly Bryant, Iowa Realty's marketing director, compared people snapping up these lots to the "Oklahoma landrush," while Mike said, "I was really surprised by how fast they went. We thought it would take a year to sell them" because of the high average price of the lots: $51,000. Prices of homes to be built in the area were expected to range from $150,000 to $500,000.[5]

By the mid-1990s, the huge success of the development was clear. Nearly three thousand people lived in the roughly one thousand acres making up the original subdivision of Country Club as well as Country Club West and Country Club Woods. The entire community was larger than at least eight hundred towns across the state.[6]

Mike's move up the management ladder continued. In 1991, he became senior vice president of the brokerage business, and the following year he was named president and CEO of Iowa Realty while Paul was named vice chairman and Bill remained company chairman. In 1995, Bill stepped down as chairman and was replaced by Paul. When Paul retired in 1997, Mike was named chairman of Iowa Realty.[7]

By that time, of course, Bill had sold his remaining interest in Iowa Realty, and when his employment contract expired, he stepped away from the company. Mike, however, stayed with Iowa Realty through its sale to MidAmerican Energy (now part of Berkshire Hathaway). He remained president, CEO, and chairman until 2015, when he retired and was named chairman emeritus.[8]

Journalist Walt Shotwell once said that Mike's father was Bill's "star back-up" because Paul successfully ran the real estate business, leaving Bill to wheel and deal. Mike was cut from the same cloth. He followed in his father's footsteps at the company, quietly handling more and more of its operations as Paul gradually moved away from management. Bill clearly understood his nephew's significance. "Having someone like Mike who knew the industry and could step in to oversee Iowa Realty was huge," he recalled. "I could rely on him to run the brokerage business and could focus on making deals." Much like his father, Mike gave Bill the freedom to do what he did best—bargain, buy, sell, and bring groups together to make things happen throughout greater Des Moines.[9]

BILL KNAPP II AND GERRY NEUGENT

Chapter Twenty-Six

Bill Knapp with his most trusted colleagues, Gerry Neugent and Bill Knapp II, 2011. Courtesy of JM Impressions.

As much as anyone Bill has known over the years, Bill Knapp II and Gerry Neugent were essential to his success, especially in the later stages of his career. Bill explained their significance candidly in 2012: "Without Bill II and Gerry, I would have gotten out of the business and gotten rid of everything twenty years ago. It's been really fun for me to work with them. They run the nitty-gritty of [Knapp Properties], but I'm there when we make deals. We work very well together, and we're usually in harmony in the end to do whatever project it is."[1]

Like his older brother, Mike, Bill II had not really considered a career in real estate, and although he eventually ended up at Iowa Realty as well, his journey there was much less direct. He followed Mike to the University of Iowa, but there he struggled, becoming more interested in his fraternity and parties than academics and frequently cutting classes. After a year of his son's poor grades, Paul told him to come home. Back in Des Moines in 1971, Bill II worked at the short-lived Harold Hughes for President campaign office in the Hubbell Building before taking a job at the SuperValu warehouse.[2]

Then came a piece of advice that turned Bill II's life around. Bill Wimer and Ed Campbell suggested that he go back to school, finish his degree, and then try Drake Law School. Bill II liked the idea and went to Paul, promising him that he would become an attorney if his father paid for the rest of his education. Paul agreed. Bill, meanwhile, told his nephew that he would hire the first family member to get a law degree (which would obviously be Bill II, if he completed law school) at Iowa Realty.[3]

Bill II followed through; he finished his bachelor's degree at the University of Iowa in 1974 and then went to Drake Law School. While there he clerked at Bill Wimer's law firm, where most of his work involved the Iowa Realty account. After finishing law school in 1977, he remained with Wimer for roughly eighteen months before, as promised, Bill brought Bill II into Iowa Realty as its corporate counsel.[4]

There Bill II was immediately thrown into the deep end. Unlike most young in-house attorneys, who would have been "in the back room doing research," he recalled, "I was given more opportunities right away. Paul Knapp and Bill Knapp did so many real estate transactions . . . they let me do much more than most lawyers would be allowed to do." Given Bill's trust in Bill II, a routine soon developed that lasted for decades.[5]

"Bill made deals on napkins and notecards," Bill II once said of his uncle. "He never cared for details and never carried a briefcase. . . . and he was the best rainmaker in the business. He always had a new person he knew who was interested in investing or developing or buying or selling. He was the big idea guy and the relationship guy. My job became to note the specifics, document the deals, and draft the contracts. I carried the briefcase."[6]

Jim Hubbell III, the former chairman of Hubbell Realty, said of Bill II: "For many years . . . he basically did a lot of Bill's work. Bill would come up with the deal and Bill II would wrap it up." However, as much as he liked staying behind the scenes, Bill II was considerably more than merely Bill's sidekick, recording the deals his uncle struck. According to the *Business Record*, he became widely regarded "as an instrumental, low-key type of guy known for his negotiating skills and his ability to make real estate and land development deals." It was clear to those in the know that Bill II was an essential cog in his uncle's operation.[7]

Also blessed with an aptitude for administration, Bill II rose through the ranks at Iowa Realty. He remained its corporate counsel and helped Bill more and more on the development side. In 1991, he became senior vice president of operations, directing finance, property management, and development. The following year, Iowa Realty was reorganized, and the commercial property management and development businesses were spun off into a new business called Central Properties (both remained under the Central Life Assurance umbrella), and Bill II was named president.[8]

That same year, Bill established Knapp Properties, a new firm he created and fully owned that was designed to manage his vast real estate holdings. Up to that point, the properties were overseen by Iowa Realty. But Central Life was preparing for a public stock offering, and management thought it important to separate Bill's personal real estate from the soon-to-be publicly held company. Bill served as chairman of Knapp Properties, Bill II was vice chairman and CEO, and several others—mostly from Iowa Realty—staffed the new business. When AmerUs sold Iowa Realty in 1998, Bill II moved over to Knapp Properties full-time.[9]

Meanwhile, in 1993, Mark Haviland, Bill's son-in-law and then president of the company, left his wife, Ginny, and stepped down as president of Knapp Properties. Mark and Ginny eventually got back together, but he did not return to the firm as Bill and Bill II had immediately begun looking for another person to run its day-to-day operations. They soon landed on Gerry Neugent, who became the company's president and chief operating officer that September. A native of Milwaukee, Neugent had gone to Marquette University before attending Drake Law School, where he was a classmate of Bill II's. He went on to become one of Des Moines's most respected real estate attorneys. Even better, Bill already knew and trusted the attorney, and Neugent knew a lot about Bill's real estate portfolio because he had handled much of Iowa Realty's and then Bill's legal work over the past seventeen years, first at the Wimer firm and then at the Belin law firm.[10]

Neugent seemed the ideal hire. Bill said of him at the time: "I can't think of anyone more qualified for this job. His breadth of experience reaches beyond the law. He understands the dynamics of real estate, development, and management." Bill had always needed a team behind him, and by 1999 he was convinced that Neugent was the perfect complement to Bill II: "I've never been happier, and I've never been more confident with my business life . . . and a lot has to do with these two fellows."[11]

Indeed, some of Bill's biggest developments and deals took place with the help and support of Bill II and Neugent, including the Tournament Club project in Polk City, the sale of the Staples farm and its development in West Des Moines's Jordan Creek area, and most recently Knapp Properties' commercial and residential developments of Prairie Crossing and Kettlestone in Waukee. Likewise, as Bill's philanthropic activity picked up, it was Bill II and Neugent who worked out the details of his growing donations.

In January 2008, Bill recognized the significance of his two trusted lieutenants by selling Knapp Properties to them. He also sold them each 10 percent of William C. Knapp, L.C., the major holding company of his family's immense real estate empire. Six years later, company co-owner Neugent was promoted to CEO. By that time, Bill held the title of chairman emeritus, and Bill II was chairman. Neugent became cochairman of Knapp Properties in 2018 and remained CEO, but Chris Costa, who had been with Knapp Properties since 1997 and most recently had served as executive vice president and chief operating officer, was named president.[12]

Bill Knapp II and Gerry Neugent had been with Bill for decades. Not only were they very good at the real estate business, they were two of

Bill's closest friends and associates. Loyal and trustworthy, they kept Bill's best interests at heart. But maybe most importantly, they kept Bill in the game. Bill had never been interested in retiring, and with their backing and support, he happily remained in the thick of things, dreaming up projects, meeting with people, and arranging deals.

JIM COWNIE

Chapter Twenty-Seven

Jim Cownie, 2019. Courtesy of Jim Cownie.

Bill was recently asked to describe his relationship with Des Moines businessman Jim Cownie. Was he a partner, a colleague, or a friend, a *Des Moines Register* reporter wondered? "We're just about everything," Bill replied. Indeed, despite being separated by a generation and being at opposite ends of the political spectrum—Cownie was a staunch Republican—the two grew to be close associates and business partners, with their first collaboration dating back to the early 1990s.[1]

Cownie was born in 1944 and grew up in Des Moines. After attending Dowling High School, he graduated from the University of Notre Dame, then went to the University of Iowa College of Law but dropped out after a year. He returned to Des Moines and went to work with his father in investment banking, where he expected to remain. Meanwhile Jim Hoak, a longtime friend of Cownie's, had returned to Des Moines to join the Ahlers Law Firm after serving as a legal adviser for an FCC commissioner in Washington, D.C.[2]

The two had always wanted to work together, and in 1970 they founded Hawkeye Cablevision and entered the embryonic cable television industry. They sought investors from the Des Moines business community and offered stock to the public the following year. Amid these early activities, Cownie first met Bill Knapp in 1973. The real estate magnate was on his list of people to cold-call to sell advertising to. After Cownie introduced himself and gave the Iowa Realty owner his spiel, Bill told him to stop by the office for a visit. Cownie did, and Bill bought a $25 advertising spot.[3]

After initially struggling, the cable operation broke through the same year Cownie met Bill when it won the Des Moines cable franchise. Rapid expansion followed. Cownie and Hoak changed the name to Heritage Communications, took their business beyond Iowa, and added television and radio stations along the way. Growth over the next ten years made Heritage the ninth largest cable operator in the country, before Cownie and Hoak sold the firm to Tele-Communications, Inc., for $887 million in 1987.[4]

Several years before the sale, Cownie became interested in the city's downtown redevelopment and joined the Des Moines Development Corporation. Bill, of course, had been one of the prime movers of the DMDC, and it was here that the two became better acquainted. Despite their ideological and age differences, Bill and Cownie realized that they were kindred spirits. They soon found they enjoyed working together and shared an abiding love for Des Moines.[5]

Cownie was wealthy after the sale of Heritage Communications, but he was still young and wished to remain active in the business world. After deciding against investing in other companies or buying a firm to manage, he moved into real estate because, he later explained, "You don't have the operating problems in real estate that you have in some of these other endeavors. You don't have the people disappointments that come with that. So I really like real estate, and deep down I really like building things."[6]

Cownie set up JSC Farms, Inc. (later renamed JSC Properties, Inc.), in 1988 to begin purchasing and holding land, but he recalled, "I knew what I knew, and I knew nothing about real estate." He also knew that his friend Bill Knapp had had great success in the business, and he therefore began watching Bill and his team and examining their approach. "The Knapp guys have been through this over and over," Cownie noted, "so I . . . studied at the feet of the masters." His new interest in real estate and Bill's penchant for working with friends led the two into their first business deal three years later, when they joined forces with a couple of others, incorporated Ashworth Properties, and purchased 192 acres just north of Ashworth Road at what is now Grand Prairie Parkway (formerly Alice's Road) in Waukee in 1991.[7]

This proved to be one of Bill's long-term, wait for the money investments. The deal looked to pay off handsomely, but it took over twenty-five years for the returns to begin to be realized. In 2018, for example, Holmes Murphy and Associates, the nation's largest independent insurance brokerage company, erected a two-story office building on an eight-acre portion of the property. Meanwhile, over this lengthy gestation period, Cownie and Bill grew to be close friends. "We just became more and more comfortable with each other," Cownie recalled, and more partnerships followed. Since that first investment together, the two have worked together on over twenty projects.[8]

One of their biggest and most recent partnerships had its origins in 1999, when Bill bought the six hundred–acre Baker Farm southeast of Booneville and south of the Raccoon River in Dallas County. Businessman Bob Pulver had some adjacent land, and Bill suggested they put their property together in a partnership. He eventually bought Pulver out and continued buying land in the area. Then businessman Gary Kirke joined forces in 2006, when they combined their land in northern Madison and southern Dallas Counties and formed the Raccoon River Land Company.

Several years later, in 2011, however, Bill and Kirke went their separate ways, and Bill again bought out his partner's share in the company.⁹

With Kirke out, Bill asked Cownie to join him in the land company because, Bill noted, he was "a five-star partner who was smart, honorable, and brings a lot of ideas to the table. I couldn't think of anyone else I'd rather work with." Cownie signed on immediately, explaining that Bill's invitation was "the extent of my due diligence." He was clearly joking, but his comment and Bill's suggested an ease and trust between the two businessmen. Together, the partners held 1,900 acres of land with roughly three miles of riverfront property.¹⁰

The only problem was that all the land was south of the Raccoon River and not easily accessible. Knapp Properties CEO Gerry Neugent once said, "You could be standing 1,000 yards from some of our property on highway F-90 sitting in Dallas County, and to get to it you'd have to go back into Polk, down into Warren, into Madison, and back into Dallas County" before finally reaching it. Neugent therefore spearheaded the partnership's fifteen-year effort to get a bridge constructed from Dallas County Highway F-90 across the Raccoon River. The two-lane bridge was completed in 2018, crossing the river midway between Interstate 35 and Booneville, directly south of Grand Prairie Parkway.¹¹

This new access increased the value of the property, especially with the road's recent expansion south, which now intersects with the east-west Veterans Parkway and connects to I-80. The value will go up that much more when the planned extension of Grand Prairie Parkway reaches the bridge from the north. Increased accessibility made Bill and Cownie especially bullish about the property, and they believed it could be their largest project ever. "This is going to be a big deal," Cownie noted. Bill II and Neugent agreed, thinking that the development might someday rival Bill's highly successful Country Club community in Clive.¹²

Outside of business, Bill and Cownie work closely together on philanthropic projects as well. Recently, for example, they led the way in financing the downtown YMCA's aquatic center. Years ago, in fact, it was Bill who encouraged Cownie to start giving more back to the community. "He cornered me in Financial Center's parking garage and leaned on me to give more to United Way." In reality, Cownie explained, Bill has "educated a lot of people as to the wisdom and enjoy-ability of giving money away."[13]

On Bill and Cownie, attorney Steve Zumbach observed that "they're alike in one core concept: It's all about making a profit, but it's also about giving back for the greater good. Those two together share at the highest level and have been an example for our entire community."[14]

Partners in business, partners in philanthropy, and partners in the community. Together, the two business leaders have built and bettered greater Des Moines over the past thirty years, and Bill would not have had it any other way. "I couldn't have a better partner than Jim Cownie," he said.[15]

GINNY HAVILAND AND ROGER KNAPP

Chapter Twenty-Eight

Ginny Haviland, 2015.
Courtesy of Irene Knapp.

Roger Knapp, 2007.
Courtesy of Irene Knapp.

Bill's two children were never really involved in the real estate business, although initially Bill had hoped that son Roger would join Iowa Realty. According to Irene, however, Roger wanted to pursue something on his own and intentionally failed the real estate exam several times because he had no interest in entering the field. Bill ultimately understood, explaining in the late 1990s, "I want him to do what he wants to do." Nonetheless, Ginny and Roger both had a profound impact on Bill's career. He recalled recently, "I worked all day and night as Ginny and Roger were growing up. One of the big reasons I did was to ensure that they never wanted for anything."[1]

A man of his generation, Bill had been imbued with the notion that he was to be the breadwinner, while Irene was to be the homemaker and raise their children. He became a wildly successful provider for their family, but he now regrets his constant focus on work: "If I could do it differently, I would have spent more time with my kids."[2]

Born in 1950, Ginny grew up in modest circumstances just as Bill was getting into the real estate business and two years before he took over the Hollis firm and established Iowa Realty. She remembers him as a "real hard worker" and recalls that her parents were always "saving money, not spending it." Maybe Bill's upgrade to a Cadillac in 1956 gave Ginny an inkling of her father's rapid rise up the socioeconomic ladder, but it was probably another ten or so years before she realized that her father "had money" and became aware of "the things he had done." She was and is "extremely proud" of all that he has accomplished.[3]

Ginny once told journalist Walt Shotwell that she sometimes gets recognized in public and occasionally overhears the comment, "There's Bill Knapp's daughter." Such incidents, she noted, "gave me a sense of pride. I like being Bill Knapp's daughter." Indeed, she does. Ginny has been Bill's greatest champion for years. Bill II said that Ginny was always there "to give Bill a boost," while husband Mark Haviland explained, "She has supported him through every crisis and deal and wanted his success more than anyone in the world."[4]

Ginny was just shy of nine when brother Roger was born in September 1959. Unlike his sister, Roger grew up in affluence, and after the family moved into their lavish Des Moines home on the southwest corner of Beaver and Aurora Avenues in 1965, the youngster enjoyed the upscale amenities of a backyard that included a swimming pool and a tennis court. It was an episode on that tennis court that may have changed young Roger's trajectory and altered his relationship with his father.[5]

Shortly after moving into the new home, Bill hired a tennis pro to give Ginny lessons. Roger was soon watching and began taking lessons as well.

This did not sit well with Ginny, who did not like her younger brother cutting into her instruction time, so she challenged him to a match. She thought that when she defeated him badly, he would lose interest in the game and quit taking lessons. But the six-year-old won, and Ginny decided tennis was for him, not her, and she stopped taking lessons.[6]

A natural athlete, Roger took to tennis quickly and soon began rising in its junior ranks. His newfound love for tennis now matched Bill's interest in the game, and the sport proved a bonding experience for father and son. On the court, Roger grew to admire Bill's competitiveness and drive, which he knew played a big role in his father's success in the business world. Bill, meanwhile, admired Roger's talent and determination.[7]

Bill's success made it possible for Roger, who won Iowa's high school tennis championship in both his freshman and sophomore years, to move to southern California, where he could play outdoor tennis year-round and train with former tennis great and top teaching pro Pancho Segura at the La Costa Resort. After graduating from La Jolla High School, Roger won the United States Tennis Association's amateur indoor title in 1980 and was a two-time All-American at the University of Southern California before getting his degree in public administration in 1982. While in college, he played on the Grand Prix professional tennis circuit one summer. A couple of years after graduating, he returned to pro tennis, where he played on the Association of Tennis Professionals tour in 1984 and 1985.[8]

But the grueling demands of the tour combined with his parents' troubled marriage led Roger to quit pro tennis and return home. He blamed their problems on his father's long-standing affair with Connie Wimer, whom Bill continued seeing, and came back to Des Moines to support his mother. Divorce ultimately followed in 1987, and the breakup drove a wedge between Roger and Bill.[9]

Ginny, however, saw how difficult the situation was for her father as well, and she continued to support Bill through the separation and divorce, assiduously avoiding taking the side of either parent. "Ginny wanted him to be happy and wanted him to do what he needed to do," husband Mark Haviland explained. "She handled it all with grace, maturity, and the utmost respect for both her parents."[10]

Roger eventually came around, and he and his father's shared love of sports once again provided a path toward reconciliation. After quitting professional tennis, Roger had taken a job as an assistant tennis coach at the University of Southern California. But after he married, and he and his wife, Amy, began thinking about starting a family, Los Angeles became less appealing. Bill knew of Roger's interest in leaving California and mentioned this to Michael Ferrari, the president of Drake University. As a member of the school's board of trustees, Bill knew of the institution's desire to build up its tennis program. Ferrari thought hiring former tennis pro Roger Knapp would immediately add credibility to Drake's effort to become a tennis powerhouse, and it could also tie Bill closer to the school. He therefore offered Roger the job, and Roger immediately accepted it and returned to Des Moines in 1989.[11]

Once back in Iowa, Roger and his father began rebuilding their relationship through the sport. Together, the two decided that Drake needed an indoor tennis facility to beef up its program, and to that end Bill built the $700,000 Timberland Tennis Ranch just west of where Irene lived. This would serve as Drake's home tennis courts as well as be open to the public. Roger and his assistant coach, Jonas Wallgard, served as its resident pros. The Drake tennis team did not stay there long, however.[12]

Bill was soon involved in a new Drake fundraising campaign, which incorporated, among other things, building a large arena and sports complex, originally designed to include six tennis courts. Bill helped raise money for the sports center and donated $3 million toward the multimillion dollar facility, which was ultimately named the Knapp Center. But during the campaign, plans changed, and a separate $1.2 million tennis complex was envisioned. Bill donated an additional $100,000 toward that as well. When the new on-campus tennis center was completed in 1992, Bill told the crowd at the opening ceremony: "I like this tennis facility, I like the Drake tennis program, and I really like the Drake tennis coach!"[13]

Bill and Roger continued growing close again, especially after he and Connie Wimer split up in 1992. Later that decade, they connected through another sport. This time it was golf, the game Bill had long despised because it was so slow and took hours away from doing business. But in 1996, while Bill was visiting Roger in Florida—after taking the tennis program to new heights by winning two Missouri Valley league championships, Roger left Drake in 1993 and moved to Sarasota—he found he enjoyed golf. An avid golfer, Roger wanted to share this passion with his father, and he convinced Bill to try several rounds during the trip. Bill was hooked. He realized that he had been wrong about golf. The sport appealed to his competitiveness, and he soon understood that it did not deter him at all from doing business. Deals, he discovered, could easily be cut between holes during a round of golf.[14]

Meanwhile, Roger had once again become fully supportive of his father. After Bill married Susan Terry in 1998, Roger explained his feelings. "My mom still wasn't healed, and I wanted her to go on with her life. But I'm not mad at my dad. It's always difficult when a family is broken because you're always splitting time between the two and one-upmanship keeps going on. My dad has a new family now, and I'm happy for him. You always wish your family had stayed together, but I understand that it can't always work." At the time, journalist Walt Shotwell noted "an obvious mutual affection between father and son."[15]

Ten years later in 2008, however, tragedy struck. That March, forty-eight-year-old Roger was getting ready to play golf when he had a heart attack and died. Bill was devastated. His relationship with Roger had fully recovered, and the two had remained close by telephone, regularly talking several times a week. Bill remembered, "We never ended a phone conversation without saying we loved each other," and when they were together, he added, "we never shook hands, we always hugged."[16]

Bill gradually came back from Roger's death, but as journalist, businessman, and majority owner of the Iowa Cubs Michael Gartner, who had also lost a child, believed, such a death "changes you dramatically." But, he added, it also "pushes you in directions you were going anyway." For Bill, Gartner thought, the loss led to "an altruistic rush to do good. It was as if he wanted Roger to be proud of him." In the decade after Roger's death, working on behalf of charities and giving away many more millions became Bill's priority.[17]

Nephew Bill II knew firsthand the relationship Bill shared with Roger and Ginny. "His children meant the world to him, and they coddled, loved, and respected him. Bill missed Roger terribly and struggled with his death for a long time, but Ginny remained as steadfast as ever in her devotion to Bill. She continues to be his biggest supporter."[18]

GREG ABEL

Chapter Twenty-Nine

Andrea Abel, Bill Knapp, Susan Knapp, and Greg Abel on the beach at Okinawa, Japan, 2015. Courtesy of Greg Abel.

Bill has had many good colleagues and associates over the decades, but for the last fifteen years or so, Greg Abel might be his most important friend. Abel came to Iowa in 1998, when CalEnergy, the company he led as president, purchased Des Moines–based MidAmerican Energy. The move more than doubled the size of the firm, which adopted the MidAmerican name and made Des Moines its headquarters. Once in town, Abel's first move was to schedule an appointment with the state's governor, Tom Vilsack. The meeting with Vilsack went well, and he offered Abel a valuable piece of advice: meet with Bill Knapp and Jim Cownie to learn about the local business and political landscape. Abel immediately took up the suggestion and became close to both men.[1]

Abel grew up in a working-class neighborhood in Edmonton, Alberta, Canada, and graduated from the University of Alberta with a degree in commerce in 1984. He began his career in his hometown as an accountant for PricewaterhouseCoopers, but his ambition led him to seek more opportunities. He soon transferred to the firm's San Francisco office, where he became part of its oil and gas division. One of his new clients was CalEnergy, then a small geothermal power company. In 1991, CalEnergy moved its headquarters from San Francisco to Omaha, and Abel joined the firm as its chief accounting officer the following year.[2]

His intelligence and drive quickly caught the attention of David Sokol, the firm's CEO, and Abel advanced rapidly up the company ladder. When CalEnergy bought Northern Electric in Newcastle, England, Abel was sent to run it. He returned to the United States as CalEnergy's president in 1998 and headed to Des Moines to oversee the newly merged company. Sometime that fall, Abel met Bill Knapp. Introducing business leaders to Des Moines was nothing new for Bill; he had made it a practice to get to know such figures upon their arrival in the city. But Bill recognized that Abel was special and soon believed that the Canadian was "one of the smartest people I knew."[3]

The two hit it off immediately. Maybe they were drawn to each other because of their similarities. Both were competitive, loved sports, and were workaholics. Much like Bill, Abel was hyperfocused on business; he could "gather a deep understanding [of information] really quickly." He also had a similar "knack for being able to see where something was in the present, where it needed to be in the future, and what needed to be done to get there." Yet there were differences as well. Thirty-six years Bill's junior, Abel kept a very low profile, shied away from the press and interviews, and was quiet about his political views. "It's something he holds pretty close to his chest," Bill noted.[4]

Regardless, the two became good friends, and much as Bill expected, Abel's trajectory continued upward. In 1999, MidAmerican was purchased by Berkshire Hathaway. Abel remained president, became the subsidiary's CEO in 2008, and was named chairman three years later. In 2014, MidAmerican Energy Holdings Company was renamed Berkshire Hathaway Energy, a $90 billion firm with energy subsidiaries in the United States, Canada, Great Britain, and the Philippines. Four years later, while remaining chairman of the energy operation, Abel was promoted to vice chairman of Berkshire Hathaway, Inc., and he is one of a select few being considered to succeed the company's famous chairman, Warren Buffett.[5]

But Abel remained down-to-earth and self-deprecating. As Bill's friendship with him grew, the two were soon golfing together, often with Jim Cownie. When both were in town and had the time, they played at Glen Oaks Country Club in West Des Moines or, in winter, they opted for Bill's indoor golf simulator. Bill and Susan sometimes joined Greg and his wife, Andrea, at the Abels' homes in Laguna Beach and Lake Tahoe, where the men golfed while the women took in spas, shopped, or lunched. In the fall, Abel hosted an annual bobwhite quail hunting trip at Riverview Plantation in southern Georgia for a group of close friends that included Bill, Cownie, John Putney, head of the Iowa State Fair's Blue Ribbon Foundation, and Bill Fehrman, now the president and CEO of Berkshire Hathaway Energy. Bill loved the camaraderie and conversation these excursions entailed but was less than fond of the hunting portion of the trips.[6]

Like all Bill's close friendships, though, business and philanthropy inevitably entered the mix as well. The two worked on some land deals together, and Bill introduced Abel to his favorite nonprofits. Most important here was the Iowa State Fair. After Bill had Abel out to his campsite at the fair for a number of dinners, showed him around the fairgrounds, and introduced him to Putney, the Berkshire Hathaway executive became convinced that the fair should be a recipient of MidAmerican Energy's giving program. In 2007, the company erected a wind turbine at the fairgrounds; two years later, it completed an education center at the turbine's base to highlight its interest in renewable energy. These were accompanied by a $1 million donation. Six years later, the firm pledged another $1.5 million to the fair, becoming the lead sponsor for the MidAmerican Energy Stage, a new entertainment venue completed in the summer of 2015. Bill was delighted: "As Greg always seems to do, he stepped up. I'm thrilled to have him involved in the Iowa State Fair."[7]

Indeed, Abel had stepped up for Bill in ways that went well beyond the fair. In 2008, Bill was devastated when son Roger died suddenly. Abel flew down to Florida for the memorial service in his private jet, bringing Paul Knapp, Mike Knapp, Gerry Neugent, and then Iowa governor Chet Culver with him. As Susan Knapp recalled, "Roger's death and that of Greg's father [four years later] brought the two even closer together. Bill and Greg found solace in each other as they endured their losses together. It took their relationship to a new level of compassion, love, and respect for each other."[8]

Three years before Roger passed away, Bill had begun to look back on a particular part of his life. The sixtieth anniversary of the Battle of Okinawa prompted him to think about his participation in the bloody event. These recollections led him to take up another philanthropic cause, and in 2006 he donated seventy-six acres, worth more than $1 million, to the state to establish the Iowa Veterans Cemetery in Van Meter, a town twenty miles southwest of Des Moines.[9]

Bill continued to reminisce about his time in the Navy, and in 2010 he sponsored a Central Iowa Honor Flight. He and three hundred other veterans boarded a Boeing 747 for their one-day trip to see the World War II Memorial and other monuments in Washington, D.C. The trip was special for Bill and heightened his interest in his wartime service. Preparations for the trip also led to him to reconnect with James Penney, a fellow shipmate of his on the USS *Catron*. Bill and Susan flew to Penney's hometown in Alabama to meet him in the spring of 2012 and hosted Penney and his family at the Iowa State Fair that August.[10]

Bill and Penney discussed their time in the Navy and the different paths their lives had taken following the war. They even talked about traveling to Okinawa together, but such a trip was not in the cards for them.[11]

It was for Bill, however, when Abel stepped up again. He was aware of Bill's mounting interest in his World War II experience, and in April

2015 he gave Bill a rare gift. He and Andrea flew Bill and Susan on their private jet to Okinawa on the seventieth anniversary of the famous battle. Bill could see the beach where he had landed troops and could roam the tunnels where the Japanese had hidden before attacking. It was a solemn occasion for all and brought back a flood of memories for Bill. The trip was a highlight of his life. He never thought he would be back on that beach, and it was both awe-inspiring and humbling for him to see it again. "I thought of the sacrifices many made, the many who didn't come back." He was not quite sure how he survived and said only, "I was lucky."[12]

"Greg has always been there for me," Bill noted. "He is smart, ethical, kind, and generous. He has a zest for life and a great sense of humor. I feel privileged to call him a friend."[13]

SUSAN KNAPP

Chapter Thirty

Susan Knapp, 2007. Courtesy of Planned Parenthood North Central States.

In 1988 Bill Reichardt, then Des Moines's best-known clothier, introduced his friend Bill to thirty-seven-year-old businesswoman Susan Terry. He thought the two would hit it off. The two did become friends, occasionally doing things together with Reichardt and Carole Baumgarten, at that time the executive director of the Des Moines YWCA, for example, but both were in relationships at the time and nothing immediately transpired romantically.[1]

Susan was born in Des Moines in 1951, but her family eventually settled in West Des Moines, where she graduated from Valley High School in 1970. She soon married boyfriend Larry Carley but divorced him four years later. Susan then took a secretarial job at her brother-in-law Bill Rhiner's plumbing company. It was there that she met plumber Wendell Terry, and the two married the following year. But she was too ambitious and too smart to stay in a clerical position. While at the plumbing firm, she became familiar with contractors and home building. She researched the business and founded SKT Construction in 1977, and she and her husband left Rhiner to build homes and then commercial properties.[2]

Five years later, however, Susan's life was turned upside down when her husband was killed in a construction accident, leaving her with two daughters, a toddler and an infant, to raise on her own. But she endured, kept expanding her company, and married accountant Norton Gegner in 1984. Susan was back on track. She was named an "up and comer" by the *Des Moines Register* in 1987, and the following year she was one of five recipients of the Women of Enterprise Award given by the U.S. Small Business Administration and the Avon Corporation.[3]

But then she became the focus of a federal investigation and was charged with money laundering along with her business partners, Dennis and Mary Ann Harker. At issue was $85,000 that the Harkers had not reported to the IRS and had sent to Susan to be invested in the three partnerships they shared. Susan deposited the money in her checking account gradually, always keeping the deposit amount under $10,000. This was done, the government claimed, to evade the law requiring those depositing $10,000 or more in cash to file a transaction report with the IRS.[4]

Susan pleaded innocent, explaining that she completely trusted Dennis Harker, who had been her late husband's best friend and a partner of hers for years. She also noted that a banker had advised her to make a number of smaller deposits rather than a few large ones, and she was completely unaware of the bank reporting requirement. Ultimately, she was acquitted of conspiracy to defraud the government but convicted of circumventing banking laws. She was sentenced to one year of probation and fined $20,000. Susan felt fortunate to have avoided going to prison and being separated from her children, but she was ready for a change. She and Gegner divorced, and she left SKT Construction in 1992.[5]

But the biggest and best change for her came that fall when she and Bill began seeing each other more often. Bill had long liked smart, business-savvy women. Susan fit the bill, plus, he said with a smile, "She was good looking and full of life." Susan was obviously aware of Bill's wealth and power, but she was particularly attracted to his "raw intelligence, kind heart, compassion, and his ability to relate to people." "And he was cute," she added. The friendship turned to romance the following year; as Bill put it, "I had to go through a few relationships before I found the right one." It looked like Bill Reichardt's intuition had been right all along.[6]

Bill was especially pleased that Susan got along so well with Ginny and Roger. "She has a good heart, and my whole family loved her," he explained. "If they ever needed anything, they would call her first." Likewise, Bill enjoyed a good relationship with Susan's two young daughters. Such rapport made the couple's 1995 decision to live together easier. They initially took up residence in West Des Moines's gated community of Glen Oaks before moving west to a Van Meter acreage ten years later.[7]

Besides frequently traveling together, Bill took up two new activities with Susan; both would remain important to him down to the present. After Roger convinced his father that he should take up golf, Bill and Susan took lessons together. Ever since then, Bill has played golf as often as possible. Later in his life, his most frequent golf partners were John Mauro, a former Polk County supervisor, Jim Cownie, and Mark Oman, a retired Wells Fargo executive.[8]

The other new pastime Susan brought back into Bill's life was the Iowa State Fair. Susan had gone to the fair regularly since childhood. She reveled in the horse shows and won several cooking and baking contests over the years. Bill, meanwhile, had attended the summer extravaganza only sporadically. Susan reintroduced him to the fair in 1994, and he loved it. From then on, the fair became a staple for the couple.[9]

At that first fair, Bill and Susan met John Putney, executive director of the fair's fundraising arm, the Blue Ribbon Foundation. Putney was in the midst of a multimillion dollar fundraising campaign to save and restore the fair's crumbling buildings. He gave them a tour of the grounds. Over the next couple of years, Bill's interest in the fair grew, and he and Putney became better friends. By the fall of 1996, Putney sensed the time was right to ask Bill for a gift to the foundation. Specifically, he had in mind the renovation of the Varied Industries Building. He asked Bill for $1 million, which would be the biggest donation to date. Bill liked the idea, mulled over the amount, and made the commitment the following February.[10]

That gift and the fact that the Knapps camped at the fair for the first time that summer marked the beginning of the couple's real commitment to the Iowa institution. Over the next decade, Bill gave millions more to the fair, but perhaps even more importantly, he encouraged many of his wealthy friends to donate as well. He often made his pitch from his own special campground at the fair, located just east of the Livestock Pavilion and kitty-corner from the Blue Ribbon Foundation's compound. It was here from 1998 on that Bill and Susan parked first their posh trailer and later their luxury motor home for the duration of the fair. And here, under the campsite's upscale party tent, they regularly entertained friends and colleagues, urging them to give to the Iowa State Fair. All told, Putney estimates, Bill's involvement has probably resulted in $30 million in appropriations and gifts to the fair.[11]

Bill was happy with his new life with Susan, but when they started talking about marriage in 1997, he became uneasy because of his bitter divorce. Susan raised the issue several more times, but Bill said he could not get married again. The following year, while they were vacationing in Venice, Susan drew the line while the two were dining at the Hotel Danieli's chic rooftop terrace.[12]

She told Bill that she loved him, but it was time they got married or she needed to move on. He said he just could not do it, and the two finished their meal. As they were leaving, Bill stopped by the restroom, and when he returned, he insisted that they return to the table and have their photograph taken. He then took her on a gondola ride, where he handed her a note that said, "Susan, will you be my wife?" She told him he had to say the words. Bill did, and the two were married that fall in Aspen.[13]

Some looked askance at the couple. They noted the twenty-five-year age difference, believing that Susan was a trophy wife who had married for money and social position. But those who knew them saw it differently. It was clear that they loved each other and enjoyed spending time together, whether in Des Moines, at their home in Florida, or at their condominium in Chicago, traveling internationally, or driving in their motor home to Susan's many quarter horse competitions. Bill II noted, "Susan has been great for Bill and dotes on him. She always checks in on him at the office, and she even calls him when he's on the golf course. Maybe most importantly, Susan handles all the details in his life that he hates; she schedules events, she organizes trips, she arranges parties."[14]

John Putney agreed. "Susan takes very good care of Bill. She keeps him active and interested." At the same time, he explained, Bill "is very supportive" of Susan, encouraging her "to live her dream of competing" with the finest horses at national competitions.[15]

"We appreciate and encourage each other," Susan says. "I think we both got lucky. It's been great for both of us." Bill agrees, but he may feel that he got the better end of the deal. "Susan is really something special. She is without a doubt the best thing that ever happened to me."[16]

A NOTE ON SOURCES

Much of this book is based on interviews, telephone conversations, and correspondence with Bill Knapp and people who have known him over the course of his life. They are listed below. Some of my previous books were also important, including *Covering Iowa: The History of the Des Moines Register and Tribune Company* (2000), *In for the Long Haul: The Life of John Ruan* (2003), *The Real Deal: The Life of Bill Knapp* (2013), *Constructing a Legacy: The Weitz Company and the Family Who Built It* (2015), and *A Great State Fair: The Blue Ribbon Foundation and the Revival of the Iowa State Fair* (2017).

Roger Brooks, telephone conversation with author, 5 March 2012.
Bonnie Campbell, interview by author, Des Moines, Iowa, 27 December 2011. Correspondence with author, 2 August 2019; 6 July 2020.
James Cownie, interview by author, Des Moines, Iowa, 17 September 2012.
Dave Elbert, correspondence with author, 3 June 2019.
Carly Fisher, correspondence with author, 10 July, 15 October 2018; 18 April, 5 August 2019; 16 March, 20 May, 5 June 2020.
Linda Grandquist, correspondence with author, 9, 10 September 2020.

Mark Haviland, interview by author, Clive, Iowa, 9 September 2019.

Bill Knapp, interview by author, West Des Moines, Iowa, 23 September 2010; 14 October 2011; 24 August 2012; 7 January, 13, 26 February, 23 April, 7 May, 25 June, 2 July, 11 December 2019. Conversations with author, 20 June, 17 July, 2 August, 31 October 2018; 6 December 2019.

Bill Knapp II, interview by author, West Des Moines, Iowa, 16 December 2010; 27 September 2011; 13 February, 7 May, 4, 25 June, 7 October 2019. Correspondence with author, 2 July, 27 August 2019; 15 May 2020.

Susan Knapp, interview by author, Van Meter, Iowa, 5 October 2012; interview by author, West Des Moines, Iowa, 11 December 2019. Conversation with author, 6 December 2019. Correspondence with author, 18 May 2020.

Doug McAninch, interview by author, Des Moines, Iowa, 13 August 2019.

Dwayne McAninch, interview by author, Des Moines, Iowa, 13 August 2019.

Gerry Neugent, interview by author, West Des Moines, Iowa, 30 March 2012; 13, 26 February, 7 October 2019. Correspondence with author, 19 November 2019.

Jack Wahlig, interview by author, Clive, Iowa, 30 August 2011.

Connie Wimer, interview by author, Des Moines, Iowa, 31 August 2011. Correspondence with author, 2 September 2019.

NOTES

Preface
1. Bill Knapp, conversation with author, 6 December 2019.
2. Susan Knapp, conversation with author, 6 December 2019.
3. Bill Knapp, interview by author, West Des Moines, Iowa, 11 December 2019.
4. Ibid. For context, see William B. Friedricks, *The Real Deal: The Life of Bill Knapp* (Des Moines: Business Publications Corporation, 2013). All references to this book are to this edition.
5. Bill Knapp, interview, 11 December 2019.
6. Bill Knapp, conversations with author, 20 June, 17 July, 2 August 2018.
7. Ibid., 31 October 2018.
8. Ibid.
9. Ibid.
10. Friedricks, *The Real Deal*, 118.

Introduction
1. Friedricks, *The Real Deal*, xii.
2. Ibid., xii–xiii.

3. Ibid., 19.
4. Ibid., xi.
5. Ibid., 22.
6. For the quotes, see ibid., 40, 42, 52.
7. The idea that profits from Iowa Realty home sales fueled Bill's early land development projects was emphasized by Bill Knapp II, interview by author, West Des Moines, Iowa, 13 February 2019.
8. Friedricks, *The Real Deal*, 80.
9. For the Weitz quote, see ibid., 94.
10. Ibid., 157.
11. Ibid., 168.

1. "Do What You Like, and It Will Never Be Work"
1. Friedricks, *The Real Deal*, 25.
2. Ibid., 39.
3. Ibid., 38–39, 45, 57, 66–67.
4. Ibid., 66–67.
5. Ibid., 173.
6. Ibid., 59–61.
7. Ibid., 61, 192–193.
8. James Cownie, interview by author, Des Moines, Iowa, 17 September 2012.
9. Friedricks, *The Real Deal*, xi.
10. Ibid., 174.

2. "You Can't Do It All by Yourself"
1. Bill Knapp, interview by author, West Des Moines, Iowa, 13 February 2019.
2. Friedricks, *The Real Deal*, 56.
3. Bill Knapp, interview by author, West Des Moines, Iowa, 23 April 2019.
4. Quote from Bill Knapp, interview, 13 February 2019. For more information on following up on the details of deals, see Bill Knapp II, interview by author, West Des Moines, Iowa, 13 February 2019.

5. Bill Knapp, interview by author, West Des Moines, Iowa, 26 February 2019.
6. Friedricks, *The Real Deal*, 39.
7. Ibid., 71.
8. Ibid., 75.
9. Bill Knapp, interview, 26 February 2019.
10. Bill Knapp II, interview, 13 February 2019.

3. "Build Relationships and Keep in Touch"
1. Friedricks, *The Real Deal*, 63–64.
2. Ibid.
3. Ibid., 88–89.
4. Ibid., 64.
5. Ibid., 173.
6. Ibid.
7. First quote from Gerry Neugent, interview by author, West Des Moines, Iowa, 13 February 2019; second quote from Bill Knapp, interview by author, West Des Moines, Iowa, 13 February 2019; and third quote from Friedricks, *The Real Deal*, 70.

4. "Buy and Hold Land"
1. Bill Knapp quote from Bill Knapp, interview by author, West Des Moines, Iowa, 7 May 2019, and John Grubb quote from Friedricks, *The Real Deal*, 78.
2. Walt Shotwell, *The Knapps and Notable Others: From Less Than Something to More Than Plenty* (Des Moines: Walt Shotwell, 2000), 51.
3. Quote from the *Des Moines Register*, 12 September 1990.
4. Friedricks, *The Real Deal*, 164.
5. Ibid., 164–165.
6. Ibid., 167.
7. Ibid., 162.
8. Ibid., 163.
9. Ibid., 201–202.

10. Ibid., 202.
11. Ibid., 202–203.
12. Quotes from Bill Knapp II, interview by author, West Des Moines, Iowa, 13 February 2019, and Bill Knapp, interview by author, West Des Moines, Iowa, 13 February 2019.

5. "Don't Dwell on the Past; If You Do, You Lose Focus on the Present"
1. Gerry Neugent, interview by author, West Des Moines, Iowa, 26 February 2019.
2. Ibid.
3. Friedricks, *The Real Deal*, 167.
4. Ibid.
5. *Des Moines Register*, 20 June 1988.
6. Bill Knapp, interview by author, West Des Moines, Iowa, 7 May 2019, and Bill Knapp II, interview by author, West Des Moines, Iowa, 13 February 2019.
7. Bill Knapp, interview by author, West Des Moines, Iowa, 13 February 2019.

6. "Close Deals Quickly, and Aim for a Win-Win"
1. Bill Knapp, interview by author, West Des Moines, Iowa, 7 January 2019.
2. Friedricks, *The Real Deal*, 77.
3. Ibid., xi.
4. For the quote, see Bill Knapp, interview by author, West Des Moines, Iowa, 13 February 2019, and for the Rusty Scupper deal, see Bill Knapp II, interview by author, West Des Moines, Iowa, 4 June 2019.
5. For Rupprecht buying the site and for the quote, see Bill Knapp II, interview, 4 June 2019. See also the *Des Moines Register*, 22 December 1986.
6. Bill Knapp, interview by author, West Des Moines, Iowa, 7 May 2019.

7. *Des Moines Tribune*, 5 November 1979, 8 February 1980; Friedricks, *The Real Deal*, 151; and Bill Knapp II, interview, 4 June 2019.
8. Friedricks, *The Real Deal*, 151, and Bill Knapp II, interview, 4 June 2019.
9. First quote from Walt Shotwell, *The Knapps and Notable Others: From Less Than Something to More Than Plenty* (Des Moines: Walt Shotwell, 2000), 52. For more on his attitude on doing deals and for the second quote, see Bill Knapp, interview, 7 May 2019.

7. "Don't Hold Grudges"
1. Friedricks, *The Real Deal*, 101.
2. Bill Knapp II, interview by author, West Des Moines, Iowa, 7 May 2019. On the horse track, see Randy Dwain Parvin, "Prairie Meadows: An Analysis of Gambling and Economic Development," master's thesis, Iowa State University, 1994, 27–35.
3. On Bill and Grandquist becoming next door neighbors in Napa Valley, see the *Des Moines Register*, 22 October 1989. For the partnership that bought and then sold land to Gary Kirke, see Bill Knapp II, interview by author, West Des Moines, Iowa, 4 June 2019.
4. Bill Knapp II, interview, 4 June 2019.
5. Ibid.
6. Ibid.
7. Ibid., and Marvin Pomerantz, *The Best I Can Do: An Autobiography* (Bloomington, Ind.: AuthorHouse, 2006), 64.

8. "Real Estate Is Risky: Do What You Can to Decrease Risks"
1. Bill Knapp, interview by author, West Des Moines, Iowa, 13 February 2019.
2. Ibid.
3. Bill Knapp, interview by author, West Des Moines, Iowa, 26 February 2019.

9. "Be Prepared for Bad Times"
1. Friedricks, *The Real Deal*, 150.
2. Ibid.
3. Ibid., 149–151.

10. "Court the Media"
1. Bill Knapp, interview by author, West Des Moines, Iowa, 7 May 2019.
2. Bill Knapp II, interview by author, West Des Moines, Iowa, 7 May 2019.
3. Friedricks, *The Real Deal*, 203.
4. Ibid., 203–204.
5. Ibid., 204.
6. Ibid.
7. Ibid., 204–205.
8. *Des Moines Register*, 29 January 2008.

Part 2. Where Credit Is Due
1. For the quote, see David and Elizabeth Kruidenier with Beverly Rivera Davis, *David and Liz: Dancing Through Love* (New York: iUniverse, 2007), 317.

11. Irene Knapp
1. Friedricks, *The Real Deal*, 13–16.
2. Ibid., 16–17.
3. Ibid., 21.
4. Ibid., 56.
5. Ibid.
6. Ibid., 47.
7. Ibid., 46–47, 57.
8. Ibid., 57.
9. Ibid., 139.
10. Ibid., 140–141.
11. Ibid., 141–142.

12. Ibid., 142.
13. Ibid., 142, 145.
14. Ibid., 145.

12. Kenny Grandquist

1. Friedricks, *The Real Deal*, 38.
2. Quote from Walt Shotwell, *The Knapps and Notable Others: From Less Than Something to More Than Plenty* (Des Moines: Walt Shotwell, 2000), 36. On Grandquist becoming sales manager, see Friedricks, *The Real Deal*, 39, 45.
3. Friedricks, *The Real Deal*, 45.
4. Ibid., 53.
5. Ibid.
6. Ibid.
7. Ibid., 57, 67.
8. Ibid., 71.
9. Ibid., 68.
10. Ibid., 47.
11. Ibid., 92–93.
12. Ibid., 93.
13. Ibid.
14. Ibid., 95, 100–101; *Des Moines Register*, 22 October 1989; and Linda Grandquist, correspondence with author, 9 September 2020.
15. Friedricks, *The Real Deal*, 194–195.
16. Shotwell, *The Knapps*, 40.

13. Paul Knapp

1. First quote from the *Des Moines Register*, 12 October 1987; second quote from Walt Shotwell, *The Knapps and Notable Others: From Less Than Something to More Than Plenty* (Des Moines: Walt Shotwell, 2000), 57.
2. Friedricks, *The Real Deal*, 9–10, 21.
3. Ibid., 46.
4. Quote from the *Des Moines Register*, 12 October 1987.

5. Friedricks, *The Real Deal*, 59–60, 61, 63.
6. Ibid., 92.
7. Ibid., 96.
8. Ibid., 96–97.
9. Ibid., 99.
10. Ibid., 151.
11. Quotes from the *Des Moines Register*, 12 October 1987.
12. Shotwell, *The Knapps*, 60.
13. McAninch quote from Friedricks, *The Real Deal*, 206.

14. John R. Grubb

1. Friedricks, *The Real Deal*, 24–25.
2. Ibid.
3. Ibid., 50. Quote from the *Des Moines Register*, 25 May 1958.
4. Friedricks, *The Real Deal*, 50.
5. Ibid., 51, 78.
6. John R. Grubb, *My Life: A Memoir* (Des Moines: Ink Publishing, 2000), 90.
7. Friedricks, *The Real Deal*, 43, 63–64, 89.
8. Ibid., 78–79, 138.
9. On Grubb's death and significance, see the *Des Moines Register*, 9 December 2003. Bill's quote from Grubb, *My Life*, 93.

15. Hy-Vee Food Stores

1. *Des Moines Register*, 18 February 2017.
2. Bill Knapp, interview by author, West Des Moines, Iowa, 14 October 2011.
3. Friedricks, *The Real Deal*, 78.
4. Ibid.
5. Bill Knapp II, interview by author, West Des Moines, Iowa, 27 September 2011.
6. Bill Knapp II, interview by author, West Des Moines, Iowa, 13 February 2019.

7. Quote from Bill Knapp, interview by author, West Des Moines, Iowa, 7 January 2019. On the 2013 lunch meeting, see the *Des Moines Register*, 28 February 2017.
8. Friedricks, *The Real Deal*, 112.
9. *Des Moines Register*, 28 February 2017.
10. Ibid., 11 February 2014.
11. Ibid., 7, 26 February 2017. For more details, see Bill Knapp II, correspondence with author, 2 July 2019. Quote from Bill Knapp, interview, 7 January 2019.

16. Bill Wimer and Connie Wimer

1. For the quote and more information, see Bill Knapp, interview by author, West Des Moines, Iowa, 25 June 2019. See also Connie Wimer, interview by author, Des Moines, Iowa, 31 August 2011.
2. Friedricks, *The Real Deal*, 71–72.
3. Ibid., 79, 107.
4. For Bill Wimer's role and the quote, see Bill Knapp II, interview by author, West Des Moines, Iowa, 13 February 2019. On Bill sending Wimer to southern California, see Friedricks, *The Real Deal*, 142.
5. Friedricks, *The Real Deal*, 99, 148; Bill Knapp II, interview by author, West Des Moines, Iowa, 25 June 2019; Bill Knapp, interview by author, West Des Moines, Iowa, 26 February 2019; and Gerry Neugent, interview by author, West Des Moines, Iowa, 30 March 2012.
6. Friedricks, *The Real Deal*, 138–139; Connie Wimer, interview; Bill Knapp, interview, 25 June 2019; Bill Knapp II, interview, 25 June 2019; Bonnie Campbell, interview by author, Des Moines, Iowa, 27 December 2011; *Des Moines Tribune*, 15 December 1978; and *Des Moines Register*, 18 July 1993.
7. Friedricks, *The Real Deal*, 138–140, 142–143, 145–148, 188–189.
8. On Bill Wimer's death, see the *Des Moines Register*, 18 July 1993. On Connie Wimer, see Connie Wimer, interview.

17. Jack Wahlig

1. Bill Knapp, interview by author, West Des Moines, Iowa, 25 June 2019.
2. Friedricks, *The Real Deal*, 72.
3. Ibid., 88–89.
4. Ibid., 150. For Wahlig's quote, see Jack Wahlig, interview by author, Clive, Iowa, 30 August 2011, and for Bill's quote, see Bill Knapp, interview by author, West Des Moines, Iowa, 7 January 2019.
5. For Bill II's quote and observations, see Bill Knapp II, interview by author, West Des Moines, Iowa, 25 June 2019. On Wahlig's role in the settlement with Grandquist, see Friedricks, *The Real Deal*, 101.

18. Harold Hughes

1. Friedricks, *The Real Deal*, 65.
2. Ibid., 84.
3. Ibid.
4. See Bill Knapp, interview by author, West Des Moines, Iowa, 7 January 2019. First quote from the *Des Moines Register*, 12 December 2011; second quote from the *Des Moines Register*, 14 January 1990. For Hughes connecting Bill to other Democrats, see Friedricks, *The Real Deal*, 88.
5. First quote from Walt Shotwell, *The Knapps and Notable Others: From Less Than Something to More Than Plenty* (Des Moines: Walt Shotwell, 2000), 91; second quote from Friedricks, *The Real Deal*, 84.
6. Friedricks, *The Real Deal*, 84–85.
7. Ibid., 85, 159–162, 175–182.
8. Ibid., 86.
9. Ibid. Quote from Bill Knapp, interview by author, West Des Moines, Iowa, 25 June 2019.
10. Friedricks, *The Real Deal*, 86. Quote from Bill Knapp, interview by author, West Des Moines, Iowa, 14 October 2011.
11. Friedricks, *The Real Deal*, 86–88.

12. Quote from Bill Knapp, interview, 25 June 2019. For Bill creating a job for Hughes, see Friedricks, *The Real Deal*, 152–153.
13. Ibid., 153.
14. Ibid.
15. Shotwell, *The Knapps*, 95.

19. John Ruan
1. Quote from the *Des Moines Register*, 14 January 1990. For more on John Ruan, see William B. Friedricks, *In for the Long Haul: The Life of John Ruan* (Ames: Iowa State University Press, 2003).
2. Friedricks, *The Real Deal*, 104. For the quote, see Bill Knapp, interview by author, West Des Moines, Iowa, 24 August 2012.
3. Friedricks, *The Real Deal*, 104, and Walt Shotwell, *The Knapps and Notable Others: From Less Than Something to More Than Plenty* (Des Moines: Walt Shotwell, 2000), 110.
4. Bill's quote from Friedricks, *The Real Deal*, 104. On Ruan Center being surpassed as the state's tallest building by 801 Grand, see Friedricks, *In for the Long Haul*, 202.
5. Friedricks, *The Real Deal*, 105–106.
6. On the Blair House project, see Bill Knapp II, interview by author, West Des Moines, Iowa, 4 June 2019, and the *Cedar Rapids Gazette*, 16 August 2015.
7. Friedricks, *The Real Deal*, 109.
8. Ibid., 111.
9. Ibid.
10. Ibid., 113–117.
11. Ibid., 213–214.
12. Ibid.
13. Ruan's quote from Shotwell, *The Knapps*, 111.

20. Guido Fenu
1. For background and the Waterloo quote, see Friedricks, *The Real Deal*, 107. On Fenu's significance and for the second quote, see Bill Knapp, interview by author, West Des Moines, Iowa, 11 December 2019.

2. *Des Moines Register*, 12 August 1972, 30 April 1993, and 15 February, 21 April 2013.
3. Ibid., 30 April 1993.
4. *Des Moines Tribune*, 18 October 1978.
5. Friedricks, *The Real Deal*, 107, and *Des Moines Tribune*, 23 August 1979.
6. Bill Knapp, interview by author, West Des Moines, Iowa, 25 June 2019.
7. *Des Moines Tribune*, 11 October, 8 November 1979, and 6, 20 March, 2 April, 6 November 1980, and *Des Moines Register*, 27 March 1981.
8. First quote from Bill Knapp, interview, 25 June 2019; second quote from the *Des Moines Register*, 27 March 1981. See also Friedricks, *The Real Deal*, 108.
9. For Moore's quote, see Friedricks, *The Real Deal*, 108; for Bill Knapp II's quote, see Bill Knapp II, interview by author, West Des Moines, Iowa, 25 June 2019.
10. For the first quote and more on Fenu, see the *Des Moines Register*, 21 April 2013. Second quote from Bill Knapp, interview, 25 June 2019. On Baumgarten and Fenu clashing, see Bill Knapp II, interview, 25 June 2019. And on the sale of the Savery, see Friedricks, *The Real Deal*, 188.
11. Bill Knapp, interview, 25 June 2019.

21. Ed Campbell and Bonnie Campbell

1. Quote from Bonnie Campbell, interview by author, Des Moines, Iowa, 27 December 2011.
2. *Des Moines Register*, 9 May 2010. For Campbell's quote, see Walt Shotwell, *The Knapps and Notable Others: From Less Than Something to More Than Plenty* (Des Moines: Walt Shotwell, 2000), 97. See also Friedricks, *The Real Deal*, 85.
3. Bonnie Campbell, interview.
4. Ibid. Quotes from the *Des Moines Tribune*, 9 October 1981.
5. Bonnie Campbell, interview.

6. Friedricks, *The Real Deal*, 154.
7. Ibid., 155, and Bonnie Campbell, interview.
8. Bonnie Campbell, interview.
9. Ibid.
10. Shotwell, *The Knapps*, 96; Bill Knapp, interview by author, West Des Moines, Iowa, 25 June 2019; and Bonnie Campbell, interview.
11. See Bonnie Campbell, correspondence with author, 2 August 2019. Quote from Bonnie Campbell, interview.
12. Bill Knapp, interview, 25 June 2019, and Bonnie Campbell, correspondence with author, 6 July 2020.

22. Dwayne McAninch

1. *Des Moines Register*, 20 July 2006. See also Bill Knapp, interview by author, West Des Moines, Iowa, 11 December 2019.
2. *Des Moines Register*, 31 August 1987.
3. Dwayne McAninch, interview by author, Des Moines, Iowa, 13 August 2019.
4. Ibid. For the quote, see Doug McAninch, interview by author, Des Moines, Iowa, 13 August 2019.
5. Dwayne McAninch, interview. See also Bill Knapp, interview by author, West Des Moines, Iowa, 7 May 2019.
6. Bill Knapp II, correspondence with author, 27 August 2019.
7. For the quote and background on the Colorado oil business, see Walt Shotwell, T*he Knapps and Notable Others: From Less Than Something to More Than Plenty* (Des Moines: Walt Shotwell, 2000), 133. See also the *Des Moines Register*, 31 August 1987, and Bill Knapp II, interview by author, West Des Moines, Iowa, 4 June 2019.
8. Bill Knapp II, interview, 4 June 2019.
9. Ibid.; see also the *Des Moines Register*, 13 November 1991. For the quote, see Doug McAninch, interview.

10. McAninch's quote in https://businessrecord.com/Content/Default/Archives/Article/McAninch-pushes-earthmoving-into-the-future/-3/988/42757. See also the *Des Moines Register*, 27 June 2006. For Bill II's quote, see Bill Knapp II, interview by author, West Des Moines, Iowa, 7 May 2019.
11. Bill Knapp, interview, 7 May 2019; Bill Knapp II, interview, 7 May 2019; Dwayne McAninch, interview; and Doug McAninch, interview. See also the *Des Moines Register*, 26 January 1983 and 1 June 2000, and William B. Friedricks, *A Great State Fair: The Blue Ribbon Foundation and the Revival of the Iowa State Fair* (Des Moines: Business Publications Corporation, 2017), 99.
12. Doug McAninch, interview.
13. Bill Knapp, interview, 7 May 2019.

23. David Kruidenier
1. William B. Friedricks, *Covering Iowa: The History of the Des Moines Register and Tribune Company* (Ames: Iowa State University Press, 2000, 126-128).
2. For Liz Kruidenier's quote, see David and Elizabeth Kruidenier with Beverly Rivera Davis, *David and Liz: Dancing Through Love* (New York: iUniverse, 2007), 337.
3. Bill's quote from Walt Shotwell, *The Knapps and Notable Others: From Less Than Something to More Than Plenty* (Des Moines: Walt Shotwell, 2000), 126; Kruidenier's quote from the *Des Moines Register*, 10 January 2006.
4. Friedricks, *The Real Deal*, 178. Bill's quote from Bill Knapp, interview by author, West Des Moines, Iowa, 11 December 2019.
5. Liz Kruidenier's quote from Friedricks, *The Real Deal*, 178. Bill's quote from Bill Knapp, interview, 11 December 2019.
6. Friedricks, *The Real Deal*, 178.
7. Connie Wimer, correspondence with author, 2 September 2019, and Susan Knapp, correspondence with author, 2 September 2019.
8. Bill Knapp, interview by author, West Des Moines, Iowa, 23 September 2010.

9. Ibid.; Kruidenier, *David and Liz*, 337; and *Des Moines Register*, 13 July 2001.
10. Friedricks, *The Real Deal*, 179.
11. Ibid.
12. For Bill's quote, see Bill Knapp, interview by author, West Des Moines, Iowa, 25 June 2019. See also Friedricks, *The Real Deal*, 182–183.
13. Friedricks, *The Real Deal*, 184.
14. For the gifts, see ibid.; Bill Knapp II, interview by author, West Des Moines, Iowa, 4 June 2019; and https://www.unitypoint.org/desmoines/article.aspx?id=1b06ee5c-1efb-4f14-a12f-5eb22bca3ffd.
15. See https://patch.com/iowa/westdesmoines/15-minutes-with-bill-knapp-when-you-die-you-dont-take-one-thing-with-you.

24. Roger Brooks

1. Mark Haviland, interview by author, Clive, Iowa, 9 September 2019.
2. Ibid.
3. Roger Brooks, telephone conversation with author, 5 March 2012.
4. For Brooks moving up in the company, see the *Des Moines Register*, 11 December 2005, and http://www.iowabusinesshalloffame.com/inductees/brooks-rogerk.html. Brooks's quotes from Roger Brooks, telephone conversation.
5. Friedricks, *The Real Deal*, 157–158.
6. Ibid., 158–159.
7. Ibid., 168.
8. Ibid., 170.
9. Ibid.
10. Ibid., 169–170.
11. Ibid., 188.
12. Bill Knapp, interview by author, West Des Moines, Iowa, 25 June 2019; Roger Brooks, telephone conversation; *Des Moines Register*, 20 September 1988; and Friedricks, *The Real Deal*, 194.

25. Mike Knapp

1. Friedricks, *The Real Deal*, 38, 45–46.
2. Ibid., 99.
3. Ibid., 151.
4. Ibid.
5. Ibid., 165.
6. Ibid., 166.
7. Ibid., 187–188.
8. *Business Record*, 16 November 2015.
9. Walt Shotwell, *The Knapps and Notable Others: From Less Than Something to More Than Plenty* (Des Moines: Walt Shotwell, 2000), 57. For Bill's quote, see Bill Knapp, interview by author, West Des Moines, Iowa, 25 June 2019.

26. Bill Knapp II and Gerry Neugent

1. Bill Knapp, interview by author, West Des Moines, Iowa, 24 August 2012.
2. Friedricks, *The Real Deal*, 99.
3. Bill Knapp II, interview by author, West Des Moines, Iowa, 4 June 2019.
4. Ibid.
5. Walt Shotwell, *The Knapps and Notable Others: From Less Than Something to More Than Plenty* (Des Moines: Walt Shotwell, 2000), 65.
6. Bill Knapp II, interview by author, West Des Moines, Iowa, 16 December 2010.
7. For the quotes, see the *Business Record*, 13 June 1994.
8. Friedricks, *The Real Deal*, 184.
9. Ibid., 187.
10. Ibid., 186.
11. First quote from the *Des Moines Register*, 24 September 1993; second quote from Friedricks, *The Real Deal*, 197.

12. *Des Moines Register*, 19 January 2008 and 28 May 2014, and https://businessrecord.com/Content/Default/All-Latest-News/Article/Costa-named-president-and-COO-of-Knapp-Properties/-3/248/80766.

27. Jim Cownie

1. *Des Moines Register*, 27 August 2017.
2. James Cownie, interview by author, Des Moines, Iowa, 17 September 2012.
3. *Des Moines Register*, 27 August 2017.
4. William B. Friedricks, *In for the Long Haul: The Life of John Ruan* (Ames: Iowa State University Press, 2003), 129.
5. James Cownie, interview, and Bill Knapp, interview by author, West Des Moines, Iowa, 13 February 2019.
6. See Kent Darr, "Now Starting at Quarterback, Jim Cownie," *Business Record*, 2 September 2016.
7. Ibid. On the purchase, see also James Cownie, interview; Gerry Neugent, interview by author, West Des Moines, Iowa, 7 October 2019; and Gerry Neugent, correspondence with author, 19 November 2019.
8. For Holmes Murphy, see https://mywaukee.com/under-construction-holmes-murphy. For the quote, see James Cownie, interview.
9. *Des Moines Register*, 27 August 2017. See also Bill Knapp II, interview by author, West Des Moines, Iowa, 7 October 2019, and Gerry Neugent, interview, 7 October 2019.
10. Bill's quote from Bill Knapp, interview, 13 February 2019. For Cownie's quote and information about the property, see the *Des Moines Register*, 27 August 2017.
11. For Neugent's quote and information about the bridge, see https://whotv.com/2017/08/24/another-bridge-for-madison-county-in-the-works-but-not-that-one. See also Gerry Neugent, interview, 7 October 2019, and Bill Knapp II, interview, 7 October 2019.

12. For Cownie's quote, see the *Des Moines Register*, 29 August 2017. See also Gerry Neugent, interview, 7 October 2019; Bill Knapp II, interview, 7 October 2019; and Bill Knapp, interview, 13 February 2019.
13. First quote from James Cownie, interview; second quote from the *Des Moines Register*, 27 August 2017.
14. Zumbach's quote from the *Des Moines Register*, 27 August 2017.
15. Bill's quote from ibid.

28. Ginny Haviland and Roger Knapp

1. On Roger failing the real estate exams, see Friedricks, *The Real Deal*, 144. Bill's first quote from Walt Shotwell, *The Knapps and Notable Others: From Less Than Something to More Than Plenty* (Des Moines: Walt Shotwell, 2000), 121. His second quote was recounted in Bill Knapp II, interview by author, West Des Moines, Iowa, 7 October 2019.
2. Bill Knapp II, interview, 7 October 2019.
3. Quotes from Shotwell, *The Knapps*, 117.
4. First quote from ibid., 118. Second quote from Bill Knapp II, interview, 7 October 2019. Third quote from Mark Haviland, interview by author, Clive, Iowa, 9 September 2019.
5. Friedricks, *The Real Deal*, 67–68.
6. Ibid., 91.
7. Ibid., 91–92.
8. Ibid., 140–145.
9. Ibid., 145.
10. Mark Haviland, interview.
11. Friedricks, *The Real Deal*, 145–146.
12. Ibid., 147.
13. Ibid., 182–183.
14. Ibid., 192–193.
15. Shotwell, *The Knapps*, 120–121.
16. Friedricks, *The Real Deal*, 205–206.

17. Ibid., 209.
18. Bill Knapp II, interview, 7 October 2019.

29. Greg Abel

1. See the *Globe and Mail* (Toronto, Canada), 4 May 2019, https://www.theglobeandmail.com/business/article-the-oracle-of-edmonton-is-greg-abel-the-next-warren-buffett.
2. Ibid., and *Des Moines Register*, 16 August 1998.
3. *Des Moines Register*, 16 August 1998. Quote from Bill Knapp, interview by author, West Des Moines, Iowa, 13 February 2019.
4. *Globe and Mail*, 4 May 2019.
5. See https://horatioalger.org/members/member-detail/gregory-e-abel.
6. Bill Knapp II, correspondence with author, 15 May 2020; Susan Knapp, correspondence with author, 18 May 2020; and James Cownie, interview by author, Des Moines, Iowa, 17 September 2012.
7. William B. Friedricks, *A Great State Fair: The Blue Ribbon Foundation and the Revival of the Iowa State Fair* (Des Moines: Business Publications Corporation, 2017), 120–121. For Bill's quote, see Bill Knapp, interview, 13 February 2019.
8. Friedricks, *The Real Deal*, 205. For the quote, see Susan Knapp, correspondence.
9. Friedricks, *The Real Deal*, 201.
10. Ibid., 210–212.
11. Ibid.
12. *Des Moines Register*, 25 May 2015. See also Susan Knapp, correspondence. For the quote, see Bill Knapp, interview, 13 February 2019.
13. Bill Knapp, interview, 13 February 2019.

30. Susan Knapp

1. Friedricks, *The Real Deal*, 189.
2. Ibid.

3. Ibid., 189–190.
4. Ibid., 190.
5. Ibid.
6. Bill's first quote from ibid. Second quote from Bill Knapp, interview by author, West Des Moines, Iowa, 7 January 2019. For Susan's quotes, see Susan Knapp, interview by author, Van Meter, Iowa, 5 October 2012.
7. Friedricks, *The Real Deal*, 191. For the quote, see Bill Knapp, interview, 7 January 2019.
8. Friedricks, *The Real Deal*, 193.
9. Ibid., 191.
10. William B. Friedricks, *A Great State Fair: The Blue Ribbon Foundation and the Revival of the Iowa State Fair* (Des Moines: Business Publications Corporation, 2017), 75–76.
11. Friedricks, *The Real Deal*, 199–200.
12. Ibid., 193–194.
13. Ibid.
14. Bill Knapp II, interview by author, West Des Moines, Iowa, 13 February 2019.
15. Friedricks, *The Real Deal*, 194.
16. Susan Knapp's quote from Susan Knapp, interview by author, West Des Moines, Iowa, 11 December 2019. Bill's quote from Bill Knapp, interview, 13 February 2019.

INDEX

Page numbers appearing in italic type refer to pages that contain photographs. Throughout this index, the abbreviation BK will be used to indicate references to Bill Knapp.

A
Abel, Andrea, *128*
Abel, Greg, 128–132, *128*
Adventureland Estates, 96
affordable housing, 77, 83
Airport Commerce Park, 96
Alcon Construction, 62, 65
Allied Development, 61–62, 65
Ankeny, 28–29, 42–43
Ashworth Properties, 119
Aviation Expo, 42–43

B
bad times, preparation for, 39–40
Baker Farm, 119
Bankers Trust, 80
Battle of Okinawa, 4, 46, 131–132
Baumgarten, Carole, 88, 133

Belin McCormick law firm, 70, 91
Berkshire Hathaway, Inc., 107, 130
Bethel Mission, 77, 102
Blair House apartments, 82
Blue Horizon Motel, Clear Lake, 20
Blue Ribbon Foundation, 97, 135–136
Breakfast Club, 20, 73, 105
Brooks, Roger, 4, 8, 38, 104–108, *104*
Bryan, Dick, 39, 77
Bryant, Kelly, 111
Burman, Jo Ann, 48
Burnett, Robert, 82
Business Publications Corporation, 71
Business Record, 70–71

business tenets of BK, 11–43
    on bad times, 39–40
    on buying land, 22–26
    on closing deals, 30–32
    on grudges, 33–36
    on help, 16–18
    on media, 41–43
    on past, 27–29
    on relationships, 19–21
    on risk, 37–38
    on work, 12–15
Buyers Realty, 25
buying and holding land, 22–26

C

Camelot West Apartments, West Des Moines, 31–32
Campbell, Ed and Bonnie, 89–93, *89*
Capital Square office building, 7, 83
Central Iowa Honor Flight (2010), 131
Central Life Assurance, 8–9, 38, 105–107, 110, 114
Central Properties, 114
Chrystal, John, 76, 92
Civic Center Court, 83
Clark, Lloyd, 95
Clarkson, Lew, 6
Cleven, Roger, 13, 53
closing deals, 30–32
Cooper, Ed, 18
Costa, Chris, 115
Cotton, William, 6

Country Club business park, West Des Moines, 66, 96
Country Club development, Clive, 23–24, 106, 110–111
Cowles Commons, 7
Cownie, Jim, 14, 37, 84, 103, 117–121, *117*
Crivaro, Pete, 83
Culver, John, 76, 90, 91

D

Daily Record, 70–71
Dalmer, Bert, 42
Daniels, Ron, 25
Davidson, Reed, 31–32
debt, 37–38
Des Moines
    downtown revitalization, 7, 66–67, 77, 81–84
    economic development of, 7–8
    post-WWII housing boom and, 5–6
Des Moines Development Corporation (DMDC), 7, 82–84, 118
Des Moines Redevelopment Corporation, 84
Des Moines Register, 42–43, 76, 78, 91, 100
Des Moines Savings and Loan, 39
Door of Faith Mission, 77
Downs, James, Jr., 39, 73
Drake University, 102–103, 125

E

economic recession (1979–1982), 8, 40, 73, 106
Edeker, Randy, 66–67
Elbert, Dave, 43
Elsie Mason Manor, 83, 91
Elwell, Denny, 28–29, 42–43

F

Farm Bureau Life Insurance Company, 24, 37
farm crisis (1980s), 22–23
Fenu, Guido, 85–88, *85*
Ferrari, Michael, 125
Fitzgibbon, John, 82
Flynn, Tom, 62, 70
Fogarty, Frank, 71

G

Galleria shopping center, 9, 25
Gartner, Michael, 14–15, 126
Gentry, Cecelia "Cee," 20–21
Glasrud, Ted, 83
golf, 14, 58, 125–126, 135
Grandquist, Evelyn, 13
Grandquist, Kenny
    contributions to success of BK, 51–55
    friendship with BK, 13–14, 34
    Iowa Realty and, 6, 17–18, 27, 52–54, 57, 73
    photograph, *51*
    Universal Realty and, 33–34, 54

Gray's Lake Park, 63, 97, 103
Greater Des Moines Board of Realtors, 20
Greater Des Moines Committee (GDMC), 81–84
Greene, Pat, 30–31
Grubb, John R.
    contributions to success of BK, 60–63
    development projects with BK, 6–7, 22, 37
    friendship with BK, 13
    Hy-Vee stores, building, 65
    low-income housing project and, 77
    photograph, *60*
    Scottish Rite Masons and, 20
Grubb, John W., 7
grudges, 33–36
Guido's Restaurant, 7, 86–89

H

Hamilton, Mark, 92–93
hard times, preparation for, 39–40
Haviland, Mark, 104–105, 114, 123
Haviland, Virginia "Ginny" (daughter), 47–48, 122–127, *122*
Hawkeye Cablevision, 118
Hawkins, Lex, 76
Heritage Communications, 118
Higgins, Tim, 42
Hilton Hotel, 84
Hoak, Jim, 118
holiday parties, 14, 104

Hollis and Company, 5, 17
Hollis, Byron, 12, 17, 61
Holmes, Linda, 54
Homes of Oakridge, 77, 102
Hotel Savery, 7, 69, 84–88
Houser, Bob, 82–83
Hubbell, James, Jr., 82
Hubbell, Jim III, 55–56, 114
Hughes, Harold, 9, 62, 75–79, *75*, 90–91
Hy-Vee Food Stores, 6, 23–24, 37, 64–67, *64*

I
I & B Café, Allerton, 4–5
Interstate Acres, 7, 22, 96
interstate routes and exits, land surrounding, 7, 22, 42–43, 77–78
Iowa Cubs, 55
Iowa Realty
    agents and employees of, 16–18
    Ankeny, subdivisions in, 28–29
    BK's purchase of, 6
    Central Life Assurance's purchase of, 8, 106–107
    expansion and franchise of, 54, 58
    profit-sharing program, 18
    real estate market downturns and, 39–40, 73
    stock ownership in, 17–18
Iowa Realty Foundation, 102
Iowa State Fair, 97–98, 103, 130–131, 135–136
Iowa Title Company, 70
Iowa Veterans Cemetery, 103, 131

J
Johnson, Lyndon, 77
JSC Properties, Inc., 119
Jurgens, Ric, 66

K
Kettlestone, Waukee, 115
Kirk, Joe, Sr., 6
Kirke–Van Orsdel Incorporated, 24
Kirke, Gary, 34, 94–95, 119–120
Knapp Center, Drake University, 103, 125
Knapp Properties, 9, 24, 25, 42, 43, 66–67, 74, 96, 114–115
Knapp, Bill II (nephew)
    on BK, 127, 137
    career, 69–70
    contributions to success of BK, 112–116
    on Guido's Restaurant, 87
    Iowa Realty and, 8–9, 17
    Knapp Properties and, 43
    on land purchases, 26
    on McAninch Corporation, 97
    photograph, *112*
    Rusty Scupper restaurant deal and, 30–31
    on Wahlig, 73
Knapp, Harold (cousin), 109–110

Knapp, Irene Hill (first wife), 4, 13, 46–50, *46*
Knapp, Mike (nephew), 8–9, 17, 109–111, *109*
Knapp, Paul (brother)
    Aviation Expo and, 42
    contributions to success of BK, 56–59
    on farm purchases of BK, 22–23
    Iowa Realty and, 6, 17–18, 53–54, 110–111
    Paul R. Knapp Animal Learning Center, Iowa State Fairgrounds, 97
    photograph, *56*
    on residential development, 106
    vacations with BK, 13–14
Knapp, Roger (son), 48–49, 69, 103, 122–127, *122*
Knapp, Susan (second wife)
    contributions to success of BK, 133–137
    on Greg Abel and BK, 131
    holiday parties, 14, 104
    marriage and relationship with BK, 9, 108, 135–137
    photographs, *128, 133*
Knapp, William "Bill"
    Breakfast Club and, 20, 73, 105
    cars of, 62, 104–105
    childhood and education, 4–5, 30
    early career, 4–5, 47
    exercise and sports interests, 13–14 (*see also* golf; tennis)
    Hotel Savery and, 7, 69, 84–88
    military service, 4, 46, 131–132
    philanthropy, 3, 10, 63, 77, 97–98, 102–103, 120–121, 130–131, 136
    photographs, *56, 80, 85, 104, 112, 128*
    politics and, 9, 20, 75–79, 90–91, 97
    real estate career, 5–6, 12, 47 (*see also* Iowa Realty; Knapp Properties)
    top 10 business tenets, 11–43
    on bad times, 39–40
    on buying land, 22–26
    on closing deals, 30–32
    on grudges, 33–36
    on help, 16–18
    on media, 41–43
    on past, 27–29
    on relationships, 19–21
    on risk, 37–38
    on work, 12–15
    vacations and travel, 13, 92, 101, 131–132, 136
Kruidenier, David, 10, 45, 82, 99–103, *99*
Kruidenier, Liz, 100–102

L

Lacy, Steve, 84
Lakeview Medical Park, 23

land purchasing, 22–26
low-income housing, 77, 83

M
McAninch, Doug, 95, 97–98
McAninch, Dwayne, 59, 94–98, *94*
McGladrey accounting firm, 72–74
Meals from the Heartland, 77, 103
media, 41–43
Meline, Tim, 107
Meredith estate, 6–7, 22, 53, 63, 69
Merle Hay Mall, 81–82
Meyer, Gene, 84
Mid-America Group, 23
MidAmerican Energy, 107, 128–131
MidAmerican Energy Stage, Iowa State Fair, 131
Miller, David, 20, 62–63, 73, 103
Miller, Herman, 109–110
Miller, Tom, 43
Moore, Gene, 87
Myles, Irene, 87

N
Napa Valley, Booneville, 24, 34, 96, 106
National Chiropractic Malpractice Insurance Company, 37
negotiating deals, 30–32
Nelson, Willie, 102

Neugent, Gerry
bridge across Raccoon River and, 120
on business deals of BK, 14, 21, 27
contributions to success of BK, 114–116
Knapp Properties and, 9, 42–43
photograph, *112*
as real estate attorney, 69–70
Neumann, Daryl, 54, 58
Niday, Clair, 59, 110
Northrup, Ed, 5

O
Odell, Mary Jane, 79
Oman, Mark, 25

P
passion for work, 12–15
past, dwelling on, 27–29
Paul R. Knapp Animal Learning Center, Iowa State Fairgrounds, 97
Pearson, Ron, 66
Penney, James, 131
Plaza condominium, 8, 83
Polk City residential development, 24–25
Polk County Courthouse Annex, 84
Pomerantz, Marvin, 23, 34–36
Prairie Crossing, Waukee, 96, 115
Prairie Meadows Racetrack, 34

present, importance of, 27–29
Pulver, Bob, 119
Putney, John, 97–98, 135–137

R
Raccoon River Land Company, 119
Raccoon River, bridge across, 120
real estate market, 39–40
recessions, 8, 39–40, 73, 106
Regency West Business Park, 35
Reichardt, Bill, 133
relationships, importance of, 19–21
Richard O. Jacobson Exhibition Center, 98
Riley, Roy, 69
risk reduction, 37–38
Rosenfield, Joe, 76, 81
Ruan, John, 7, 35–36, 80–84, *80*
Rupprecht, Dan, 31
Rusty Scupper restaurant, 30–31

S
Scottish Rite Masons, 20, 58, 62
Segin, Jeff, 42
Sheridan Park, 61
Shotwell, Walt, 111, 123, 126
SKT Construction, 134–135
Slater, Gary, 97–98
Smith, Ken, 96–97
Smith, Neal, 76
Stanbrough, Gene, 8, 30
Staples farm, 25, 115
Stoner, Tom, 62

Stuart Hills, 61–62
Swanson, Dwight, 62

T
tennis
   BK and, 14, 58, 105
   Roger Knapp and, 48–49, 69, 123–126
Timberland Tennis Ranch, 125
Timmons, Robert, 71–72
Tiny Tots Childcare Center, 77, 102
top 10 business tenets of BK, 11–43
   on bad times, 39–40
   on buying land, 22–26
   on closing deals, 30–32
   on grudges, 33–36
   on help, 16–18
   on media, 41–43
   on past, 27–29
   on relationships, 19–21
   on risk, 37–38
   on work, 12–15
Tournament Club of Iowa, 96, 115
Traditions Golf, 24–25
Trumbull, Harold, 65
Turner, Beatrice, 48–49

U
United Investments, 53
United Way, 121
Unity Point Health, 37, 55, 103
Universal Realty, 33–34, 54

V

Vaudt, David, 43
veterans, 103, 131–132
Vilsack, Tom, 129
Vredenburg, David, 64–65
Vredenburg, Dwight, 65–66

W

Wahlig, Jack, 21, 39–40, 72–74, *72*
Wallgard, Jonas, 125
Wandro, Mark, 42
Weitz, Fred, 7, 62
Wells Fargo Home Mortgage, 25
West Bank, 20, 63
West Glen Town Center, 34
West Lakes Business Park, 23–24, 27–28, 96, 106
Westchester Manor, 96
Wilkey, Richard, 34
William C. Knapp Charitable Foundation, 102, 115
Wimer, Bill, 17, 68–71, *68*, 113
Wimer, Connie, 9, 49, 68–71, *68*, 78, 92, 101, 102
work, attitude toward, 12–15
World War II, 4, 46, 131–132

Y

YMCA, 84, 120

Z

Za-Ga-Zig Shriners, 20, 62
Zelda Acres, 61
Zimpleman, Larry, 84
Zumbach, Steve, 121

www.ingramcontent.com/pod-product-compliance
Lightning Source LLC
Chambersburg PA
CBHW031320160426
43196CB00007B/600